APHS

Photograph of Bearer.

ssage
r the
of the

CANADIAN HEADQUARTERS
LONDON

Signature of Bearer.

National Registration Code.	EKFG	186	6

Names of Children (under 16 years of age) accompanying holder.

(CABIN CLASS)

IMMIGRATION IDENTIFICATION CARD

THIS CARD MUST BE SHOWN TO THE EXAMINING OFFICER AT PORT OF ARRIVAL

Name of passenger _____ HIBBERT _____ Joyce K.

Name of ship _____ SCYTHIA _____ 13

Name appears on Return sheet _____ line _____ 4

Medical Examination Stamp

Civil Examination Stamp

(See back)

The War Brides

The War Brides

edited by Joyce Hibbert

PMA Books

Canadian Cataloguing in Publication Data

Hibbert, Joyce, 1923-
   The war brides

ISBN 0-88778-185-3

1. Wives—Canada. 2. Canada—Emigration and
immigration. 3. World War, 1939-1945—Women.
I. Title.

HQ759.H53   301.42'7'0971   C78-001517-7

Design: Michael Solomon

Peter Martin Associates Limited
280 Bloor Street West, Suite 306, Toronto, Canada M5S 1W1

To all the women who married Canadian servicemen during the Second World War and as a
group became known as the war brides.

Contents

Preface

War brides was the popular term applied to British and European women who married Canadian servicemen during the two world wars. I became a war bride when I married a Canadian soldier in March 1945.

This book is about the 48,000 war brides of the Second World War, the great majority of whom were natives of the British Isles.

Due to the shortage of transport, only a few women came to Canada during the war, but from 1945 to 1947 bride ships brought the women and children across the Atlantic in hundreds and thousands. From special trains the young women spilled out at train stations in cities, towns and whistle stops across Canada. Despite the pangs of homesickness and the weight of culture shock, they settled down and, except for the few who returned home, they were gradually absorbed into Canadian life.

For several years I mulled over the idea of a book about their lives. Barry Broadfoot's *Six War Years* provided inspiration, and I decided that a first-person format might work for a book about the war brides. That was in 1975—International Women's Year. The time seemed ripe to contact the war brides.

Nostalgia was in the air, and I found that the women were ready to tell their stories. They wrote about their wartime experiences, their encounters with Canadian servicemen, their memorable journeys to Canada and the hardships and joys of those first few years.

The stories in *The War Brides* recreate the war and the postwar years from a special perspective. Most of the women who speak in this book are now ordinary Canadian citizens, but their romantic journey—both physical and emotional—to their new land and the courage, humour and determination that marked their adventure sets them apart. It makes them Canadians and equally important, women with a special story to tell.

Joyce Hibbert

Introduction

"Bring back a real English lady."

Advice to a Canadian Army private
from his father, in a short story
printed during the war.

DURING the war there began to flourish in Canada a sort of sub-literature that faded soon after V-E Day along with the innocent and elderly generation that produced it. Thumpingly patriotic and Empire-minded, its chief contribution was to render unbridgeable the gap that already existed between men overseas and the civilian population at home. This gap, or fissure, was as profoundly psychological as physical for it separated two kinds of experience, the real from the sentimental. It had been created in part by the songs and movies dumped in Canada as second-hand patriotic fodder; by the rather dainty propaganda issuing from Canadian sources, notably the National Film Board; and by tons of romantic misinformation filed by correspondents operating abroad. The war had become a myth while it was still a passage of history; the civilian attitude to the women Canadian soldiers married overseas has to be seen in the light of this myth-in-progress.

Consider a story about an overseas courtship published during the war. Bud, an inarticulate and not very bright Canadian private becomes engaged without the least difficulty or opposition or even much effort to the wealthy, young and beautiful Lady Clarissa. Clarissa's father shows no curiosity about Bud or about the future to which he is committing his only child. Instead of asking a pertinent question or two he uncorks champagne and proclaims his faith in the Empire—"building a bridge" is what he calls this alliance. Before the end of the story Bud manages to put a whole sentence together: his father owns half of Canada, including "a railway or two". As Bud was embarking with his regiment, he recalls, his father said, "Bring back a

Mavis Gallant was a journalist with the Montreal *Standard* in 1944 and covered the arrival of some of the war brides.

real English lady." Obviously an important segment of society has been missing until now in that rough corner of Empire—refined womanhood; the reader is left with the feeling that Lady Clarissa will be the first in Canada of her kind.

This was a story written by a Canadian, for Canadians, some of whom probably did not find it preposterous simply because it took place within the myth. Bud (the knight who was really a prince) and Clarissa (daughter of a grateful sovereign) meet in a fairy-tale kingdom very far from Canada indeed. Looking for "a real English lady", supreme wartime souvenir, Bud stood for the soldier civilians wanted to see; by stepping over the chasm to a legendary Old Country he became transformed. In the wartime novel, *Remember Me* by Edward Meade, two Canadian privates in England wonder why they cannot find the thatched cottages their English cousins have been sending them on Christmas cards for years and years. How much is allowable fantasy and how much is a lie? True to their generation, the Canadians cannot decide.

That was one aspect of the legend. Another took the form of anecdotes. English girls, avid for marriage, were said to leap on any passing Canadian and drag him into blacked-out doorways for goings-on too shameful to describe—the soldier meanwhile clinging to a lamppost and protesting, "No, no, I'm engaged to a nice girl in Regina!" Torn from his lamppost and his chastity the Canadian, as the expression went, "had to marry her". Stories embroidered on this pattern increased as the number of overseas marriages multiplied. It was widely repeated that the Army encouraged such marriages in order to keep the men docile and to prevent them from deserting or getting drunk and shooting up Aldershot. I doubt if many people at home knew about Canadian Army Routine Order 788 and its bleak reminder, " . . . the general policy is to dissuade members of the Canadian Army from a marriage in foreign lands", or would have believed it if they had been told.

From the beginning of the war unmarried Canadian

women were assigned a role: "the girl back home". They were assured they would gather lilacs, that there would be bluebirds and that the absent "you" of the songs would be back. In time it became apparent that lilacs were indeed being gathered, but by someone else. Standards of female conduct were offered as a sop: the insufferable Mrs. Miniver, or the wife of the RN captain in Noel Coward's *In Which We Serve* who when asked by her husband—who had been posted missing—if she had worried about him replies, "Of course not, I've been much too busy." (Of the unnatural, the fatuous, the witless behaviour that was demanded of women not nearly enough has been said.) A great many women lived lives that were lonely and isolated, affected by the war and yet not part of it, dependent on mail, with real life—as they imagined it—indefinitely postponed. Word drifted back of the superior quality of women *there*: they had suffered, Canadians had not; they were good sports, easy to get along with; they had an advantage said to be lacking in Canadian women—they understood men. Recipients of this news—now assigned a new role, "the girl I used to know"—understood that "wonderful women" would soon be followed by "wonderful girl I've met", followed in turn by "married".

A number of somewhat floundering studies tried to explain why these marriages were taking place, and it was here that fact and legend began to fuse. Marriage *there* carried an echo of historical reality, a proof of participation in a war civilians were still inclined to see as romantic. The truth was obviously simpler. A two-liner of the period probably had it pat: "What has she got that I haven't got?" "Nothing, but she's got it here." The girls cast off could only go on hearing descriptions of the pluck and high spirits of those characters of fiction who had turned into real rivals, and continue to accept the harping accusation, with its flavour of inflicted guilt, dished out by war correspondents and returning Canadians: "You people don't know what hardship means." Hardship, like expectation, has its own fever chart. War brides arriving in Canada often wondered what sort of reputation had preceded them. Canadians probably ought to have been wondering what sort of Canada had been offered to them. If it was true that the idea civilians had of the war and of life in Western Europe was miles from the truth of it, men overseas (irritated by civilian obtuseness, as one was frequently reminded) painted for their brides a highly idealized picture of the Canada they had left behind—a picture enhanced by home-sickness, youthful memories and the passage of time. How very long that passage was seems to have been forgotten. Europeans still know nothing about it, any more than they realize how large the contingent was in proportion to Canada's small population. In fact, the long dislocation of an entire generation would be disastrous for some of the men and women in it. Canadian men were the first to go, the last to come back, and there were an awful lot of them.

More than forty-one thousand Canadian soldiers married overseas, mostly in Britain. Towards the end of the war their wives—so-called war brides, a term some of them detested—began to arrive in Canada along with some twenty-one thousand children. Even for a nation built on the principle of immigration it was an unusual wave: all one generation, all women, nearly all from the same racial stock. A foreigner reading this volume might be led to think they were also uniformly educated and that they had found themselves, almost to a woman, plunged in a primitive culture that was inferior to anything they had known. Of course something like that did take place; the accounts provided are eloquent. Most of the brides had grown up in towns and cities and might have been just as daunted by life on an English or Scottish farm, few of which were any more modern or comfortable than those in Saskatchewan. The trouble was that no one had warned them or explained exactly what is contained in the words, "prairie winter". To a great many of these women the cultural poverty of their new surroundings was devastating; the wonder was that they stayed. But to make the picture complete and clear it must also be said that there arrived a number of women who were giddy, or silly, or who wanted to get away from home, who were emigrating for a lark, who had married too young and too fast; and there were some whose backgrounds would have seemed limited even by the most humble Canadian standards. The shock for Canadian families receiving them was often very great—as great as that felt by brides who found they had married into families where the only conceivable use for a book was as a doorstop.

The brides were issued with Canadian cookbooks; it would be interesting to know what was in them. The recipe for something more practical than pumpkin pie was probably in order, though there is no real preparation for anything as radically different from Europe as the North American continent. No European except for a Russian can ever take in the size of Canada except by travelling across it, preferably by train. A long plane journey gives some idea, particularly at night when the lights of cities are like rafts in what seems to be the emptiest and darkest of seas. A European's first impression is often of immeasurable physical solitude. I did not know until I had read this book how dirty and uncomfortable Canadian trains seemed to the war brides, or how monotonous the land appeared on the other side of the sooty windows, with its miles of unchanging vegetation and unbroken colour patterns. To this strange, wild, entirely other scenery they were expected to respond at once, and to come up with reactions satisfying to Canadians. Travelling on a special train of war brides from Halifax as a young and ignorant reporter I kept asking them to comment on what they saw. We were in New Brunswick, in a drenching rain. Nearly every aspect of the Canadian landscape struck me as moving and poetic then, for reasons that were historical or literary or had something to do with Canadian painting and which were at a remove from the land itself: a field was not a field—it was a Goodridge Roberts. I foolishly expected a reaction tuned to mine. "What does it look like to you?" I asked tense and exhausted women, many of whom had not travelled much even in England.

"It looks rather like Surrey," said one poor bride, in desperation. Of course, it does not; I could not understand then that she had nothing to match it to.

All emigration is based on misapprehension; so is every welcome. The only German bride I encountered told me much later that she had not been on Canadian soil more than an hour before she was asked, "What do you think of the Canadian way of life?" and of the anxiety she felt, knowing that her future probably depended on the right answer. She also secretly wondered how there could be a way of life in a country whose past was so recent—another common misapprehension, for which newcomers pay dearly. A number of brides got down from their special trains at whistle stops in Quebec. Here, if anywhere, the new arrival wanted more than a cookbook (and in English at that!) while her new family would have needed a stout dose of practical reality and open-mindedness. What was probably required was a meeting of saints. One bride found that although she had lived in France, spoke fluent French and was Roman Catholic it still wasn't enough; another took thirteen years to learn enough French to be understood. The surprise is not that a few marriages cracked, but that most of them survived.

No marriage should begin under the roof of parents-in-law; many of these did. One admires the women for sticking it out. It takes only a small amount of imagination to hear the ominous, "That's not how *we* do things *here*," which makes an outsider of the son's wife once and for all. There were factors the bride could not be aware of. Sometimes the husband's parents had to face, cope with and conceal from the bride the fact that their son had thrown over his Canadian girlfriend, the one with whom they had shared his overseas letters and already considered a daughter. For the soldier the matter was settled; his parents were left holding the baby—sometimes literally. Canadians were still close to the Depression; the questions the brides heard shouted by workmen along the railway—"Has your man got a job?" and "Where do you all think you're going to live?"

—were urgent and immediate. There was a real fear in 1945 that there were not going to be enough jobs to go round; as for living quarters, the expression of the period was, "They'd begrudge you the room for your own grave." From the moment every one of the brides heard, "Has your man got a job?" a myth was dispelled. The Mrs. Miniver image now seemed commonplace, which was not the fault of the new arrivals, who had never asked for that to begin with. They would not be the first immigrants from England to learn that they were British and splendid until they unwittingly put their foot in it, on which they were shortened to Brit. The returning airman who would not abandon his RAF-style moustache or his service lingo for the next twenty years, the blackout beauty with upswept Betty Grable hair, doing her nails as the Canadian landscape rolled by, were by the summer of 1945 already type-cast and dated, like survivors from a jolly film about the war. Canadian ambivalence to Britain was never more marked than just then, as the tide of sentimentality began to ebb, leaving elderly Anglo-Canadians stranded on prewar memories, unable to place English girls who did not seem English enough, and who brought with them a disconcerting glimpse of a socialist future. It was impossible for some Canadians to understand why Churchill had lost the first election after the war. In a discussion that took place in my presence, a new bride said, "Naturally I voted Labour. What has Churchill got to do with the working class?" If she had been foul-mouthed her husband's parents could not have been more upset and horrified. The idea that they had a daughter-in-law who was going to say such things *in Canada* was more than they could live with. The mother-in-law asked me not to write what her son's bride had said about Churchill. "You can see how we'd feel," she said. "After all, we own our own home."

One of several stories circulating at that time had a war bride taken out on a lake and drowned by her husband's family. Everyone knew someone who knew where it was supposed to have happened and how and why it had been hushed up. A new folklore was created about brides who had believed they were marrying rich men (Bud and Lady Clarissa again, in an imaginary sequel) and who found themselves in slums, cabins, shantytowns, on reservations and even in igloos. "And so she turned around and went right back," these stories concluded. But one doesn't need an igloo for strangeness; a peaceful suburb can be quite enough, given a husband who was one man in uniform and quite another in civilian clothes ("He looked like Al Capone," recalls one ex-bride in this book) and with an idealized Canada falling apart. As for "She went right back," how many could or really wanted to? Only a minority, if figures mean anything. Canada had provided passage one way; not many had families who could afford to send the fare home. Some of these girls, who were very young, knew they might never see their parents again. Cheap and easy air travel was barely imaginable. England was as remote as if they had emigrated by sailing ship, while economic difficulties created a second ocean. Reading the account of the lonely young woman who could not afford a five-cent stamp to write to her mother one feels a stab of shame, as if the whole country had been found wanting. The excuse was this: nobody knew. A few who could not conquer their homesickness did go back, probably to discover that the England they returned to was already not the England they'd left. (No national returning ever finds the situation improved, but is convinced it has gone downhill steadily from the moment he departed.) Some, deeply unhappy, stayed because they did not want to hear their parents say, "I told you so."

Most war brides, I think, were helped and welcomed, but I can remember interviewing one—a grave, quiet, self-possessed girl from Scotland—who had arrived into an atmosphere of such demonic intolerance and hatred that I was actually afraid for her. Her husband, unwilling to choose between his bride and his psychotically possessive family, some of whom actually slept in the same room as the young couple, sat in an armchair, looking defeated, fiddling with the dials of a radio. The next day I went back to see her, uninvited and without a professional excuse. I did not tell anyone what I was doing, for this was known as "getting involved", which was a sin against the Holy Ghost. I talked to her, standing in the dark hall of that haunted, evil flat and offered to try to borrow the money to get her out of it. She did not reject the offer out of hand, or reproach me for my impertinence, but considered the possibility calmly. The fact that I did not have the money myself but would have to raise it (if, indeed, I could) may have weighed in the balance; but what she told me was that she would never go back on her word—she meant her marriage vows—and that as long as she could stand on her two feet she would manage. She would find a job and she would drag that beaten, jobless husband out of his armchair and into a home of their own if it killed her. She said, "He's a good boy," the "boy" deciding his civilian status in terms of reality; she had probably met him in officer's uniform, giving orders. I don't know what became of her. She is not in this book, though there are some who sound not unlike her. It is probably to them that it should be dedicated.

Mavis Gallant

The War

> When Chamberlain's announcement that war had been declared came over the radio, my mother started to cry. I couldn't understand why. To me, it was exciting. Then the sirens wailed. . . .

At first there was only an atmosphere of expectation, a vague feeling that something important was about to happen. But gradually the war touched everyone's life. The men went off to fight, and the women—housewives, shop-girls, waitresses, factory workers, typists and professionals—stayed behind to keep the country running.

For some it meant coping with rationing, bombings and blackouts —and the dread that fathers, brothers, husbands and friends would not return. Others joined the services or took up the jobs the men had left behind.

In Britain and on the Continent the future war brides were caught up in the wartime terror—and the excitement. They were young, and to them war was a great adventure. They were eager to do whatever they could to help the war effort.

The war? It was one long string of fear-filled nights in damp places where you laughed and joked to keep your spirits high. In between were the surprisingly happy times when a concert or a Vera Lynn song was like a message from heaven. And there were those blessed quiet spells in the bombing lulls when you slept a sort of desperate sleep.

Early in the war I lived in a sector that was a frequent target for air raids. Many a night the air raid siren went, and I had to run down the street in my pyjamas toward the underground shelter.

On one particular night warnings alternated with all

clears, and we had to stay put in the shelter. A lot of people played cards. Around 1:00 a.m. yet another warning sounded, and this time we got it hot and heavy. The vibration of the bomb blasts kept knocking us off our wooden seats. Suddenly there was a great WHOOMP, and we were thrown to the floor like flies swatted by a giant hand. Candles went out and dirt began pouring in through the cracked ceiling. My face was bleeding through torn skin; someone's steel helmet had struck me on the head when it flew across the shelter.

There was panic and screaming at first in the pitch darkness. And the smell of whatever bombs are made of.

I remember lighting candles with unsteady hands and remarking, "It's all right, that one was down the road." Soon we were singing. There were no more close ones that night, but we were buried in there.

It was hours and hours before we heard the sounds of digging. We yelled and cheered when a chink of daylight appeared, followed by a soldier's head. "Gor Blimey," he exclaimed to another rescuer. "They're still alive!"

We emerged from our almost tomb at 8:00 p.m. Never was the world, even with the surrounding devastation, so divinely sweet.

Another night I was going home from a late theatre show and got caught in the cross-fire of a surprise air raid. I found myself in the middle of a large area that had been bombed and then levelled off. There was only one small brick wall for protection. Hands over my head, I lay as close to it as possible. Shrapnel whined and spat blue sparks around me as it hit the cement. In my summer dress and sandals I prayed hard and loud, really loud, because I never thought I'd live through that raid.

The next afternoon, out of curiosity, I retraced my steps. On the ground were dents in the soil where I'd pressed my body, and the brick wall was covered with shrapnel pock marks. Why wasn't I hit? I can never explain it. One of the miracles of war, I suppose. I truly believe a lot of us found God, I mean really found Him, during those awful times.

During the war I lived in York and trained for teaching. York was relatively peaceful despite the war; only a few explosive bombs and a scattering of incendiaries were dropped there.

The enormity of the war effort was brought home to me when the massive air strikes against Germany started. For hours each evening the sky was full of bombers, and during the early hours of the morning we could hear them droning back to the fifteen airfields around York.

The most profoundly moving thing I saw was a group of photographs outside a newspaper office showing emaciated bodies piled high in a German concentration camp. Those photographs, plus stories of gassing and the incineration of so many people, gave me a deep understanding of the monstrous evil forces against which we were fighting.

When the war broke out I was on holiday at my parents' flat in London. I remember the frantic digging of trenches and air raid shelters in the parks. We soon had to carry gas masks everywhere.

Except for the nights spent in air raid shelters, the war didn't affect me personally until 1941, when I took a job in a village near Cheltenham, Gloucestershire, working for a blind clergyman and his family.

I had a diploma in agriculture and looked after their huge garden and I also acted as secretary to the clergyman. As the rest of the staff gradually left for war duties, I was left to do everything. The clergyman's two sons and a daughter were in the army but were home frequently. I was treated like one of the family and became engaged to one of the sons. He was killed later, in Iceland.

When evacuees started coming to the country from London, I turned the top storey of the house into a flat. Mr. Leon Goosens, a famous Belgian oboeist working with the BBC and his family were billetted with us.

We were on the route of German bombers as they flew to the Midland industrial towns, and there was a good deal of incendiary bombing. I well recall the terrible night when Coventry was bombed. We all spent the night under the dining-room table and the place shook as though there were a long, long earthquake. Ack-ack guns nearby added to the commotion. Some Gerries were shot down and several roofs of village houses were set alight by fire bombs.

Later, when the clergyman died, I moved with the Goosens family to Sussex, since my parents' flat had been bombed and all our possessions lost. I applied at the Labour Exchange for some kind of war work. They sent me to Hastings where a government agency had taken over the municipal park, the glasshouses and 200 acres of farmland north of the town. That was in 1942.

I trained Land Army girls to plant and care for vegetables. Maize, tomatoes, parsnips, carrots, turnips, onions, Brussels sprouts and other vegetables were grown for consumption by Canadian troops.

Hastings seemed full of Canadian soldiers, many of them billetted in the large hotels along the sea front. I lived with my boss's secretary near the park, and we were bombed out at two different locations. Luckily neither of us was home either time.

As the men were called up, I was given more responsibility and promoted to foreman. This meant I was in charge of three huge greenhouses and the boilers that heated them. When time permitted, I continued to work in the fields. I had to work on Sundays and late at night stoking the furnaces with coke to keep the heat even.

I dreaded the night bombings, especially when I was on duty at the glasshouse furnaces surrounded by all that glass. The glass shone in the moonlight making an easy target, and several times we had near misses and a lot of glass broken. On the way home I'd often have to lie against a wall to avoid flying debris.

During the days we were occasionally strafed by German planes as we worked in the fields. We'd either roll under a large wagon or take to the nearest ditch. One girl lost an ear and another was wounded in the leg in different raids. But somehow we got through those awful days and nights.

During the Second World War, I worked at a grocery store in my home town of Arnhem, Holland. Occupying German soldiers would often ask Dutch girls for dates. Sometimes it was hard to find a strong excuse to put them off, but I managed.

As the Allied armies advanced, the Germans decided to evacuate civilians from strategically located Arnhem. At first I stayed with my mother, brother and sister near Hilversum in North Holland province. Because of the food shortages we had to move after a few months. We were taken by night across the Ijsselmeer by boat. Then we had to walk for six hours to a camp where we were sorted out. On account of my work I was assigned to help some Dutch people who owned a grocery store at Bolswerd in Friesland province.

It was terrible to see Arnhem when I returned at the end of the war. It seemed there was nothing left intact. Everything was smashed, damaged or stolen.

According to my diary of the time, there was a proclamation in Britain on January 13, 1943, calling up women born between June 1922 and December 1923.

On return from a holiday in North Wales on October 2, I found that my final papers had arrived. As a deferred member of the Woman's Auxiliary Air Force I was ordered to report to Horsham, Sussex, for duty with the Royal Observer Corps (ROC).

From then until the war's end, I was to be engrossed in the most interesting job of my life. I worked in the ROC centre at first, alternating between four hours on the operations table and four hours on the long range board. At the table we'd receive plots from the outdoor posts in our area;

at the long range board we received plots direct from neighbouring ROC centres. Between the two, we kept track of the movement of all aircraft, friendly and hostile. From our operations room, information was passed on to the RAF.

There were occasions when we watched "hostiles" on the table plotted as being over Horsham, while at the same time, we felt the earth shaking from their bombs.

Six months later, I became a "spotter", rather than a "plotter" and was assigned to the post at Peacehaven, Sussex. It was designated L4—for call-in purposes, "Love Four". Love Four was manned mostly by World War I veterans who did Observer Corps duty in addition to their regular jobs and by those who were medically unfit for the Forces. I was told that I was the first woman to serve on an outdoor post on the southeast coast of England. Shortly afterwards two others joined me.

By day, we'd track the hundreds and hundreds of American bombers and fighters on their way to rendezvous for the massive daylight strikes on the Continent. By night, often near dusk, we watched those unforgettable hordes of Lancasters and Halifaxes heading across the coast at incredibly low altitudes of between two and three thousand feet. There was much consternation on the post one evening when an American ack-ack battery on Telscombe Tye opened up—apparently on our own bombers. Sometimes it was possible to count those outgoing bombers as they roared over, but often we'd have to resort to reporting 200 plus, 500 plus and so on. When the planes returned it was great to see or hear them going back to base. We'd be extra careful when reporting the stragglers, especially those with feathered props or damaged fuselages.

It was our duty to report every plane we saw or heard in the sky. But our post had also been installed with Snowflake rockets, which were to be launched should we spot any Germans landing. I worried more about having to send up one of those things than I did about seeing the enemy. I used to imagine myself going up with the rocket!

There were a lot of exciting times and some quiet periods

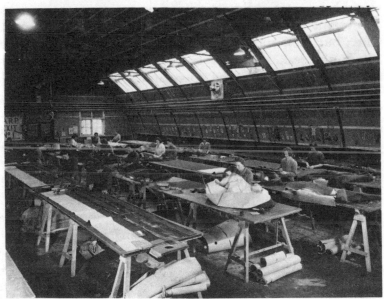

Factory work was essential to the war effort. Here women
assemble barage balloons in an RFD factory shed. A cartoon of a
cigar-smoking Churchill hangs suspended above the women.

on the job. I can't recall being afraid, because we were alert and busy if any "hostiles" were about. Then, too, we were not on the main path of German bombers or in Doodlebug Alley.

However, my girl friend and I were reduced to terror by those wretched flying insects known as June bugs. For a time around D Day, they'd swarm up to our look-out tower in the evenings. Out of the downland grass and gorse bushes they rose in squadrons, carrying out their own invasion to the accompaniment of our girlish squeals and screeches.

During the war my mother kept one hammer near the front door and another handy at the back door. This was in case a German was parachuted onto the South Downs and decided to pay a call. She was alone, but I doubt if anyone would have got past her. We lived on the edge of the open downs and always knew when a German was around. Often our milk and bread were stolen from the doorstep before daybreak, and later in the day we'd notice troops and/or police searching the downland.

The war affected almost every aspect of our lives. Sometimes it was just an annoyance. For instance, my husband, one of the Queen's Own Rifles of Canada, had bought me a new dress with black market coupons. I happened to be wearing it downtown when a low-flying Messerschmidt sprayed the street with machine gun bullets. My husband threw me down on the ground and himself on top of me. When I got up I found that I'd ripped the front of my precious new dress beyond repair. Being in the Auxiliary Territorial Service (Artillery) I was not issued clothing coupons for larger items. The loss of that dress amounted to a major personal disaster at the time.

But that was minor compared to the time we caught a German plane in our searchlight. Hit and about to crash, the pilot flew it, machine guns blazing, straight down the beam toward the light. The plane crashed and burned with

The WAAF Company from Wellesbourne, Warwickshire. British women wanted to "do their part", and many of them joined the Women's Auxilliary Air Force.

the pilot still in it. Of the ten girls on duty, no one was hurt. The only damage was one scratched steel helmet. After it was over we gathered up shells as souvenirs.

Experiences like these made me heartily resent being told by newly arrived American soldiers how they already had, or were about to win the war for us.

Wallasey in Cheshire was my home. After leaving school I tried hairdressing, library work and took a secretarial course. At seventeen and a half I joined the Women's Royal Naval Service and took six weeks of instruction in motorcycle riding at Earls Court, London. Standards were high and only the brave emerged as despatch riders.

My first ship was H.M.S. *Nelson* in Portsmouth. There were ten of us despatch riders, and we were fortunate enough to fall heir to the Admiral's cottage near Fort South-

wark. We found out later that we were living very close to the Supreme Headquarters of the Allied Expeditionary Force. General Eisenhower, of course, was commander-in-chief.

Our driving covered most of the south of England, west to Plymouth, east to Dover and north to South Wales. We sometimes drove over 450 miles, night and day regardless of weather conditions. After three months of night driving, we were awarded wings to be worn on our sleeves. That made us very proud.

On one such trip I had to carry a despatch to London for Admiral Stark of the U.S. Navy. Taking the main highway from Portsmouth to London, I found myself facing a prolonged hairpin bend at Liphook. On one side of the bend was a deep ravine, and many never made it round that curve which was known as "The DR's Graveyard". Coming in the opposite direction was a Canadian Army convoy led by another despatch rider. My speed would have been about fifty-five miles per hour and we hit head on, he on his big Harley Davidson and I on my 350 Ariel. His gas tank was dented; my bike was a write-off.

Despatch Riders maintained the military communication system when telephones and telegraph messages were judged security risks.

I was lucky enough to come out of it with only a bruised pelvic bone, but he had his face split open by my steel-tipped boot as I went over the handle bars. Then his bike fell on him and broke his ankle.

We were taken to a Canadian hospital. He had the ankle set and I was under observation for eleven days. I remember that when they wheeled him in to see me he laughingly remarked, "Next time I meet a WREN despatch rider, I'll park my bike and climb a tree until she has passed." He had just married an English girl and had been expecting to cross the Channel any day. Thanks to our collision he could spend a little more time with her.

We often escorted VIPs to and from the flagship. On one of these occasions I managed to goof again. I was standing by my bike, at attention, waiting at Fareham for Lord Nuffield. I expected to see him arrive in a large limousine, but instead, a small chauffeur-driven car pulled up and a smiling Lord Nuffield opened a window and said, "You may proceed." All went well until three miles from the dockyard gate. Then I discovered I'd lost His Lordship in the traffic. Panic stricken, I doubled back and was greatly relieved to locate him. We drove on to the flagship *Victory* where Admiral James and a guard of honour were assembled. After introductions he excused himself and came over to me. "You girls are doing a wonderful job," he said, "and we will not say anything about what happened back there." Once again I was relieved.

The war years were what you made them. We ran to air raid shelters and were bombed out, but I must say that those years were fun for the younger crowd.

Even rationing was a challenge; getting hold of an extra coupon or some scarce commodity was cause for celebration. I remember being on a bus with my weekly egg ration, a single egg, in my pocket. The bus swayed and my precious ration was squashed. And we used to enjoy some great steaks, until my husband found out they were horse meat. We soon switched to Chinese food.

In December 1940 I was reading the magazine *Woman's Weekly* when a recruiting notice for the Women's Auxiliary Air Force caught my attention. I sent the coupon off to London and in a very short time came a reply. Would I please report to an address in Southampton for an interview. Nothing ventured, nothing gained, I thought, and off I went.

I was interviewed by a smart, business-like WAAF officer who requested my qualifications. I told her I could type ten words a minute and didn't say a word about my nursing experience, as I desperately wanted to try something different—something with more than a day and a half off a month. I inquired whether I might train as a teletypist. Likely she stifled a laugh but she was very polite and suggested that I might like to work as an RDF operator. RDF stood for Radio Direction Finding, later known as radar.

After a medical I was sent to Gloucester for initial WAAF

training. This consisted of endless lectures on all aspects of
Air Force life: how to salute officers; the correct way to
wear the uniform; what one could and could not talk about
in public places, and so on.

I had mixed feelings about it all, wondering if I'd done
the right thing, especially on the day we were issued our
brand new uniforms, plus brown paper and string with
which to pack every stitch of our civilian clothes to be sent
home. The dreadful issued panties were soon dubbed
"blackouts". But the shoes were to give us the most trouble
and pain. They were heavy black oxfords, and we had to
wear them at all times. Fellow WAAFs and I returned from
many a route march in tears, with blood oozing from our
heels and grey lisle stockings stuck and caked. As the
weeks went by our feet toughened, but those shoes never
softened.

Although we hated it at first, we even got used to square-
bashing—parading early each morning in full marching kit.

Then a dozen or so of us were sent up north to Cranwell
for training as RDF operators. We worked around the
clock, staring at cathode ray tubes in little dark cubicles. At
last I had the RDF mastered and was able to make the echo
on the tube disappear.

We were allowed to give our preference for posting, and I

was lucky to go to a radar site at Worth Matravers, a few miles from my home town Weymouth, Dorset. While there, we spent a lot of our spare time on the beach at Swanage and had the scare of our lives the day a German aircraft buzzed us and dropped a bomb on the old wooden pier. In our panic we couldn't find the way out through the iron anti-invasion barricades. After that, we didn't enjoy our swims as much and made sure we knew the exact location of the exit spot.

News came that five of us were to be posted to North Wales. It was a new station and we were to be billetted in private homes in the little town of Abergele. We were miserable about leaving our Swanage friends, but these partings were an occupational hazard of life in the Services.

The morning after we arrived we were taken to see the radar site and were met at the station by a jovial bunch of Canadians, all volunteers like ourselves. Little did I know that the airman sitting next to me on the transport going back to billets would one year later be my husband.

My home was a few miles from Birmingham at Sutton Coldfield, Warwickshire. I spent almost four of the war years in the Auxiliary Territorial Service (ATS), the bulk of the time at Parsons Barracks, Aldershot.

My first impression of Aldershot was a forest of khaki uniforms, the majority of them being worn by Canadian soldiers. At first we girls were scared to walk downtown alone, but we soon found out that Canadians were normal young men and began dating them.

ATS girls were trucked to various dances organized by the Canadian Army. The dances were fun, and we met a lot of really nice boys. Their style of dancing certainly contrasted with ours! There seemed to be an awful lot of using one leg more than the other. I could hardly hobble around the day following my first evening of dancing with Canadians, but after some practice I got used to the difference in style.

The first time I asked my parents if I might take Reg, my future husband, home on leave with me, the response was,

"Yes, by all means bring him home—after all they are helping us to fight the war. But don't get any ideas in your head about marrying one of those foreigners."

Meeting Their Men

Encounters between English girls and Canadian servicemen were inevitable: the Canadian men were easygoing and friendly and didn't wait for formal introductions. A solider might strike up a conversation on a bus or train. He'd offer to carry a suitcase or push a bicycle. Or he'd ask a girl to dance and then teasingly mimic her accent.

But if any of these meetings led to marriage plans, the couple faced formidable barriers set up both by civil and military bureaucracies. The Canadian Army was particularly discouraging:

Records of marriages contracted abroad from the last war show that a pitifully small percentage turned out to be reasonably happy; it is hardly to be supposed that the experiences of the present war will be happier. In considering whether permission to marry should be given, COs and Comds will therefore bear in mind that the general policy is to dissuade members of the Cdn Army from marriage in foreign lands. If both parties are domiciled in Canada, the advantages of waiting until they return home should be pointed out. Marriage with a person from a different country, particularly by young soldiers, and where there are differences of race, religion and customs, is open to obvious risks to future happiness, and it is important that every reasonable effort be made by COs, with the help of the Chaplain, to protect them from improvidence and impetuosity. With this object in view, consent should be refused outright if the authority concerned is not satisfied that a reasonable base for a happy marriage exists.*

*Canadian Army Routine Order 788, Permission to Marry—North West Europe.

*Judging from the number of European women who married Cana-
dian servicemen between 1939 and 1945 — some 41,000 by that time
— the Army's general policy of dissuasion appears to have been
largely unsuccessful. These couples were young and determined and,
despite the obstacles, they were getting married.*

For a while the war didn't affect us very much. And then
the boys from the village started going away, and soldiers
from other parts of England arrived.

I worked at the head office of a grocery chain, something
like Dominion here. In the early days of the war they had
divided England up into areas and had a stockpile of tea in
each area so that if one was bombed, we wouldn't lose the
whole lot. If we hadn't had our tea, you know, we would
have lost the war.

Every day when I went to work, I would see the results
of the bombing from the night before. Sometimes a whole
street would be wiped out and they'd be digging people
out. That was when it started getting through to me. Then
we started to get news that a local boy was killed or missing. That was too much. I couldn't stand it any longer, so I
decided to join up, too, in the WAAFs.

I was stationed at Eastbourne for quite a while, and there
were an awful lot of Canadians there. There were so many
men and so few girls that we had half a dozen dates every
night. A lot of the Queen's Own were stationed there, and
we would tell each other how they behaved on a date. If
they got too fresh, we wouldn't go out with them.

We used to go to the Winter Garden to dance. Gordon
Ryder led the band there, and it was the most popular place
in town. There were many Canadians, and the girls used to
chase them because they had a supply of chocolate bars,
tins of chicken and salmon and other things we couldn't get
during the war. They also had lots of money so they could
take us out.

One night at the dance, I got cheesed off at the way the Canadians could have their pick of the girls. I was telling a girl friend that all you needed was Canada on your sleeve and a chocolate bar in your pocket and you would be all right. Then I looked out of the corner of my eye and saw a soldier standing next to me with Canada on his sleeve. He'd heard every word I'd said. He'd come over to ask me for a dance, but after hearing that, he didn't know whether he should or not.

That was how I met my husband. I really fell for that guy —head over heels in love—and I followed him all over England.

Love goes on whether there's a war or not. We were together as much as possible, and our time spent together was really precious. There was a sense of urgency about the whole thing; you never knew whether you'd be there tomorrow.

I had a young sister-in-law whom I dearly loved. She was killed in a London air raid, and I went to pieces over her death. My parents sent me down to the country in Surrey to get over it, and I found a job there.

One day a girl I had met there asked if I'd like to go on a blind date. At the time I thought she meant I would be going out with a blind man! She felt it would do me good to date, as I was still upset about my sister-in-law.

I took one look at my blind date, a handsome Canadian soldier, and fell for him hook, line and sinker. We dated every night, but I was still very unsettled. Without telling him, I packed in my job and disappeared back to London and my parents. It wasn't long before he turned up at our house. We talked, with all my family listening, and he asked my parents if he could marry me. My mother said that she didn't want me going to Canada where the Indians might cut off all my hair! I retorted that I could do as I liked because I was over twenty-one.

We married without official permission, and my husband

was absent without leave. That was in 1942. I should have known better but I was so in love.

We had to get married all over again so that I could get the army allowances, and my husband was confined to barracks for weeks.

I met my husband at a party given by one of my girl friends.

I'd lost the man I'd intended to marry, and Henry was alone, too, and lonesome for his folks in Canada. We remained casual friends for some time. I found out later that he had watched me many times in the High Street, sat behind me in the cinema and even followed me home to find out where I lived.

If I'd known, I'd probably have been as nervous as the dickens. You see, first off, I didn't like Canadians. I even said they were a bunch of gum-chewing hillbillies who propped up the doorways of our little town. Boy, I've eaten those words since.

Romance blossomed in army posts, at dances, in hospitals— wherever Canadian soldiers and young British and European girls met. Chance encounters often led to the altar.

My husband and I first met under a huge holly tree.

I had trained my small dog to walk with me through the common to the bus, wait until it arrived, then cross the road and go home on her own. On this particular day I was perturbed to find heavy barbed wire, army truck after army truck arriving and guards posted. I tried to send the dog home, but she refused to go and darted about. A guard tried, too, asking as he tried to catch her, "Will she bite?" Now that was silly: except for his eyes, there wasn't an unprotected inch on the man—he was wearing a steel helmet, battledress, cape, the lot.

We didn't meet again for six weeks and then he helped me rescue a kitten. He confessed that, although he'd been away on two long trips, he'd hunted for me each time he returned.

He turned up unexpectedly again after nearly a year on the Continent. I had arranged with neighbours that they should leave their bundles of laundry beside my car. Then I would deliver them to the laundry when I drove my father to catch the London train. So there I was, with five or six bundles of laundry, parents and a man just returned from God alone knew what horrors who wanted to get married.

Well, the registrar couldn't marry us that day. At least the delay gave me time to get rid of the laundry, and my father was able to phone relatives and friends. My brother and uncle somehow made arrangements for a wedding breakfast at the local hotel, but it was first come, first served. We were allotted one bottle of beer per man and one bottle of wine to three or four women. Our honeymoon lasted one week before my husband's leave was up and he returned to Holland.

My home was in Cowfold, near Horsham in Sussex. I was unable to join the forces or do war work because I suffered from asthma and related allergies. So at the time I met my husband, I was looking after four children instead. Their mother, who'd been my teacher, had died in 1942, and their father was a colonel in the British Army. I suppose I was helping the war effort.

I met my husband in February 1943 at a whist drive held at a Women's Voluntary Services canteen. He was a despatch rider with the Royal Canadian Army Service Corps and once had the honour of conducting the car of King George VI.

Needless to say, my fast-moving courtship and marriage caused quite a stir in our village. You see, I was nearly thirty-three and my husband was thirty-six. The villagers thought I'd taken leave of my senses!

I was born in Rotterdam, Holland, and when I was twelve I moved with my mother and my brother to a suburb of The Hague. During the fall of 1944-45, my mother and I had to evacuate within forty-eight hours. The Germans had decided to launch the V2s from there, and everyone had to leave.

We loaded our bicycles with suitcases and bags filled

with as many of our personal belongings as possible. The rest had to be left behind. There was no transportation available, and we had to travel on our bikes for about thirty-five miles to Schiedam, near Rotterdam. My brother had married and lived in a three-room apartment there. He and his young wife made us very welcome, and we shared everything. We often had to go by bicycle to farms and barter for food. They didn't want money, so we'd trade our possessions. Towards the end of the war one couldn't even find food to buy with ration coupons.

My husband was one of the Canadian liberators of Schiedam. He served in the First Division, Third Brigade Service Corps attached to the Ninth Field Ambulance. It was in one of those ambulances that I tasted my first cup of real tea in five years. Just wonderful!

It was love at first sight when I met my husband. I was on my bike. He was on his motorcycle. We said hello and he asked, "Can you speak English?" I mumbled, "A little bit." Actually I was one of the fortunate ones, for I'd learned three foreign languages. The English and French came in very handy when I landed in Montreal with my five-month-old son in September 1946.

One evening in January 1941 a girl friend and I were walking on the cliff side of the South Coast Road, a few miles east of Brighton. We met two rifle-carrying Canadian soldiers in battle dress coming in the opposite direction. The men were on patrol.

"You can't walk on that side of the road after dark, girls," declared one of the Black Watch of Canada types.

"Let's see what you can do about it," I shot back, always braver when another female was present.

We made a date that night to meet the following Sunday afternoon at the same spot, neither knowing what the other looked like. That was how I met my husband in the black-out, and he has been putting up with my cheek ever since.

Strictly speaking I was not a war bride but I did first contact my husband-to-be during the war.

I was a cook in the Women's Auxiliary Air Force stationed at Wrexham in North Wales. One of my WAAF friends was corresponding with a Canadian soldier whom she'd met while on leave. In one of his letters he asked her to find a pen friend for his chum.

At the time I had just scalded my foot with boiling soup and was in sick bay with lots of time on my hands. When my friend came to visit she brought me Gerry's address. It was the spring of 1944, and we wrote to each other while he went through Italy, France and Belgium. By the time VE Day arrived, he was in Holland.

At the war's end the RAF was reorganizing. I was posted several times and ended up in Grantham, Nottinghamshire. At this time the Canadian troops were being steadily repatriated. Mail service, even in the hectic transient war and post-war period, functioned remarkably well, and Gerry soon had my latest address.

One evening, I was travelling back to camp after having spent a day off in Nottingham. There was a lone Canadian soldier on the bus and something told me that it was Gerry. My girl friend and I sat at the back of the bus giggling our fool heads off. I was nervous and too shy to ask him if he *was* Gerry and I couldn't really tell by the one photo I had.

When I got back to the WAAF guard room there was a message for me. A Canadian soldier was waiting for me in the main guard room. The other WAAF and I went to meet him. There, waiting for me, was the soldier we'd seen on the bus. He's kidded me later for taking along a chaperone on that first date.

Gerry spent his leave in Grantham and we dated when I was off duty. During this time he told me that he loved me and asked me to marry him. I didn't believe in love at first sight and I certainly wasn't sure that I wanted to go to Canada. I was an only child and quite happy at home.

When his leave was up he returned to Aldershot where he awaited repatriation to Canada. I was able to get leave and went home to Winchester which wasn't far from Aldershot. We managed a few more days together before he sailed for home on the *Queen Elizabeth*.

We promised to write to one another and vowed that if it turned out to be true love we'd find a way to meet again. That was in October 1945. He stopped writing after Christmas, and I thought he'd met someone else.

About a year later I received a letter saying that he couldn't forget me, and he'd figured out a way to get back to England. If I was still interested in him, would I let him know.

Well, I was still interested all right, and we started up the correspondence again. He confessed that, after demobilization, he had spent all his money foolishly and had stopped writing because he could see no future to our relationship.

He re-enlisted in the army and, in 1948, got a berth on a grain ship which was sailing out of Fort Churchill bound for England. We were married in October and spent our four-day honeymoon in Brighton.

It was in 1942 while I was teaching at Riseley in Berkshire that I first met, and later became engaged to my husband, who was a gun sergeant in the Royal Canadian Artillery, Thirteenth Field Regiment.

Strangely enough our introduction had been pre-arranged by my cousin back in Saskatchewan. I had corresponded with her regularly since the age of eleven, and she had given my address to him when he left for England in 1941. They had lived on neighbouring farms and had gone to school together. He was naturally curious to find out what her English cousin was like. He must have liked what he saw: we were married at Christ Church, Reading, Berkshire, on October 1, 1943.

My husband saw me on a street in York one afternoon and decided he would like to meet me. He got his chance later

that same day when I was escorted to a dance by my brother. No need to say that my brother was pleased to get rid of me. Little did he know that he had just met his future brother-in-law.

Alec was a flight lieutenant in the Royal Canadian Air Force, 102 Squadron, stationed at Pocklington. We were married on VE Day. It was a rushed wedding as he was due to leave for Canada within the week to go on to the Pacific for raids over Japan.

My younger sister's fiance, who served in the RAF, was due home on leave for their wedding that same week. She had her wedding dress, veil and cake all ready for the event. She generously let us borrow the lot, and my mother had to rush off another order for a second wedding cake. My younger sister, my older sister and I were all married within a period of seven weeks.

My future husband was one of three Canadian brothers serving overseas. They came to my home town of Stourbridge, England, to look up their father's English relatives. I was away serving in the Women's Auxiliary Air Force at the time, but they came to know my family because my brother was their cousin's best friend. Apparently my future husband fell in love with a coloured photograph of me in uniform which my mother had on display.

On their next leave I returned home to be bridesmaid to my best friend. That was how Clyde and I met. He was more reserved than most of the Canadians I knew, but after four days acquaintance he asked me to wait for him. He feared that that I might be snatched up by one of the many young men on the RAF station.

In 1944 we planned to marry. All winter, on my precious days off, I worked on a white wedding dress, three bridemaids' dresses and my going-away outfit. Then at the end of March all leaves were cancelled. Later we found out that it was because of the preparations for D Day. Fortunately, if WAAFs could show proof that weddings had been planned in advance, we were granted leave. But what was I to do

about my Canadian soldier bridegroom who was on exercises somewhere on the south coast of England?

Plucking up my courage, for I was shy then, I asked to see the station commander. Now he was on a par, or almost, with the Deity in our lives. He proved to be very human and considerate, even asking me what I thought he should do. On inspiration I blurted, "How about sending one of those 'signals' the officers are always talking about, sir." He remarked that I didn't know what I was asking, but he took down all the information about my husband-to-be.

The signal must have got through because, in spite of all leaves being officially cancelled, Clyde turned up for the wedding.

There was a dance hall known as the Templars in my home town of Paisley, Scotland. That was where I first met my husband. He was in the Royal Canadian Navy and his ship was docked at Greenock about thirty miles away. We used to get some good bands at the Templars, and I think he came in that night with boys who'd been there before.

We met early in 1941 and were married in November 1942. At the time I was working at Coates Thread Mills, where we made uniforms, parachutes and other equipment.

He was away at sea a lot, but his ship usually docked at Greenock for repairs so we were together quite often. Every time he came home, my mom, who loved him, would get the kettle on for "a wee cup of tea and some toast". When we came to Canada my husband had his tea and toast every night before he went to bed.

The war was a happy and exciting time for me. Just out of my teens, I lived in Lewes, an old market town in the South Downs, where girls outnumbered boys five to one. I found myself with the patriotic duty of entertaining the troops.

When Canadians arrived to be billeted in our town, nightly dances became the rule. For the first time in my life, men pushed and jostled for the pleasure of dancing with me and begged to escort me home. Our homes were

opened to these young men with their strange accents. Some returned, some wrote a letter or two afterwards, but most of them were just passing through. They were grateful for our hospitality, but there were much bigger things on their minds.

It was June 1941 when the manageress of the NAAFI canteen invited me to a dance at Telscombe Village. We were to travel by army lorry with NCOs from the Fusiliers Mont-Royal—a daring adventure because parents warned us to be especially careful about associating with French Canadians. It was only later that I realized that of all the soldiers to be billeted in the big house opposite my sister's hairdressing salon where I worked, the FMR were the cleanest and most gentlemanly.

On Wednesday, June 9, I walked into the canteen and stared at one soldier who later manoeuvered a seat next to me in the lorry and changed my life.

The FMR, of course, was a Roman Catholic regiment, and the Padre's favourite sermon was: "Don't marry an

English Protestant girl. Sleep with her if you must, but don't marry her."

For six months after our engagement, Jean and I tried to get permission from the commanding officer to marry. But he was adamant. Finally, Jean was sent for his pre-OCTU (Officer Cadet Training Unit) exams with the British Army. Results showed that he, the youngest entrant from his unit, was the only man who had passed and qualified to enter the OCTU exams. It then occurred to us that the commanding officer's previous threat to prevent such an entry if we married was no longer valid. It was out of his hands.

Hurriedly we arranged with the old Irish priest, Father Flanagan, to be married within two weeks. And just in time! Shortly afterwards priests and clergymen were forbidden to perform such ceremonies without the commanding officer's permission and blood tests.

On February 1, 1942, we were wed, but our brief honeymoon was cut short by a telegram. Jean was to return to his unit. His commanding officer was furious and told my husband that he would never be an officer in *his* regiment.

On March 5, Jean sailed for Canada to instruct cadets at Brockville. His commanding officer had found a way to keep him from OCTU and then the anger was directed at me. I was sought out at a dance and informed by the commanding officer that I would never see my husband again. Then the Padre omitted to send in my name as a dependent, and I received no army allowance.

Having discovered that I was pregnant and facing the possibility of being unable to work full time, I wrote to Canada House in London. Soon afterwards my allowance arrived and a correspondence began with regard to the possibility of transportation to Canada.

My home was in Worthing, Sussex, and I met my husband at a local hotel where I'd been invited to a party. He introduced himself and, after an hour or so, informed me that I would like living in Canada after we were married. They were fast workers, those Canadians.

In 1942 my best friend married someone she'd met at the Beaver Club in London. Missing her company, I decided to apply for evening voluntary work at Gattis YMCA in the Strand. After obtaining references and being interviewed, I was allowed to work between 10:00 p.m. and 7:30 a.m.

One night along came these funny-looking guys with wedge caps and yellow gaiters and belts. I asked what they were and was told "Provost". One thing led to another, and one of them said, "My friend would like to meet you." So I gave him my phone number, got a call and arranged to meet the friend outside Woolworths in the Strand.

The usual question came up: "Where shall we go?" There was a good show playing at the Elephant and Castle, and he asked if I knew the way? Well, of course I did, I said. We got on the tube and promptly went in the wrong direction and had to go back and start again!

There followed many dates and shows, some of them at
Covent Garden. Then I found an apartment at Victoria, and
we used to creep in and out. When I left to get married in
December 1942, the owner who liked me said, "I saw you,
you know, but you were always with the same soldier."

Our marriage was planned for December 5, but he was
posted to Edinburgh. At first I stayed in Victoria, and he'd
get escort duties which brought him to London frequently.
We'd filled in forms and had been interviewed by his commanding officer and my dress, cake and so on were ready
for the wedding. Then one day, a guy came with a note
from Mac informing me that I'd have to live in Edinburgh
for thirty days prior to the ceremony. Off I flew to Edinburgh on a fast train and that weekend I found a place to
live and had the banns published. Then I rushed back to
London, resigned from my job and broke the news to my
shocked mother. Then up to Edinburgh again, exhausted.

The Edinburgh city police arranged the wedding. And so
I was married.

Although we'd gone ahead with the wedding, official
approval didn't come through until March 1943. What
should we do? As it stood, I was not eligible for the wives
allowance. There was nothing for it but to get married

again, this time with the blessing of the Canadian authorities. The ceremony took place at the Caxton registry office, and consequently I possess two legal marriage certificates.

For a time I worked at Canadian Military Headquarters and then in 1944, on D Day to be exact, I found that I was expecting. After our son was born, life wasn't quite the same. It was hard to find a place to rent in London; people were not interested in tenants with a baby. We finally found a place. Our bed there was the box-spring type, broken and held up by the family Bible!

Mac went to Germany, and I took my baby and went home to mother for a while, and after that, to Wood Green until March 1946 when I sailed for dear Canada aboard the *Mauritania*.

There were a lot of remarks from people at home when they found out that I was engaged to a Canadian. In short the message was, "No good will come of it." It was especially true of English servicemen returning to my home town on leave. "How could you?" one of them asked me. I was very angry with him, but I guess there was a certain amount of understandable bitterness on their part. They could see that so many of their countrywomen were choosing foreigners as mates.

My husband was a fitter-armourer with 408 Squadron, RCAF and stationed in Yorkshire. He worked on Lancaster bombers.

We met at the weekly dance held in Northallerton Catholic Church Hall in 1943. When I first took him home I recall that my mother said, "I hope this isn't serious." I replied, "Oh no, I wouldn't want to go all that distance to a strange land."

Well, after a few months we were married, and Canada didn't seem like a strange land any more. I think my sense of adventure had taken over.

I met my husband during the coffee hour after an evening church service. We went out together for a year before marrying. He used to bring me dates, tea biscuits, cake and other things that were scarce or unobtainable for civilians. At Christmas we guiltily feasted on a delicious fruit cake sent from Canada by his old girl friend.

In 1943 my husband's regiment was sent to Scotland for special training. I didn't see him for four months, but he wrote nearly every day. By this time we were planning to be married as soon as he could get leave. Suddenly there was a phone call. He'd been granted three days embarkation leave. It might be the last chance to get married until after the war....

I made all the arrangements. I didn't have a wedding dress or anything—I just wore my best dress. I hadn't the clothing coupons for new things, but I did know a dressmaker who quickly made me a nice lightweight coat from a brown blanket. And I bought a hat to match.

We were married on August 13, 1943 at the registry office. No flowers or wedding cake, but we did have our photo taken afterwards. The next morning I went as far as London with my new husband. We walked two miles in the pouring rain. My new hat shrank, and I was so mad that I threw it away! We said our goodbyes and I wasn't to see him again for twenty-six months. The regiment sailed for Italy where my husband was slightly wounded but rejoined his regiment.

Then one night there was a knock on the door and there he stood, home on two week's leave. The silly old maid I married and suggested that my husband sleep in the bath tub. We said, nothing doing! After two weeks he returned to duty in Holland where he escorted prisoners-of-war back to Germany.

Meantime, I corresponded with his sister and also tried to find out as much as I could about Canada in general, and the kind of life I'd lead, in particular. My husband planned to farm in the Ottawa region.

I was the ripe old age of seventeen, reasonably fresh from school, when I met my future husband on the only blind date of my life. I had of course been fully instructed on the perils of such behaviour by my parents, but this night in February 1943, I threw all caution to the winds!

He was in the 1st Light Ack Ack and saw action all the way up through Italy and then in Belgium and Holland. We corresponded regularly, and I was often teased by my mother who remarked that ours was a very peculiar court-ship carried on, as it was, through the mails. Just after VE Day Barrie came back to England. We became engaged on May 16 and were married on August 19, 1945.

After a honeymoon in Scotland—the Canadian Army and the Royal Navy paid our rail fare—Barrie was duly sent back to Canada.

Then followed the period of waiting and wondering. I felt that I was neither fish nor fowl. I was married, but to whom? My friend, who subsequently went to Toronto, and I had many discussions as to just what we had done by marrying men we hardly knew and preparing to leave all

that was dear and familiar for a life in a land completely unknown. We went to a brides club each week, where we were shown films and given lectures about our new country, and these were a help. But the fears still crept in. What had we done?

I'll never forget that cold grey morning in October 1947, as I stood on the deck of the *Aquitania* and asked myself for the umpteenth time, what am I doing here, anyway? Could a simple thing like getting married eight months ago have cause to put me on a ship that would transport me away from family and homeland to Canada—a country I'd never seen? As Lands End disappeared on the horizon and I turned to look at the handsome Canadian beside me, I knew it could.

I had met Bill Shaw two years previously, at a dance held at the town hall in Worthing, Sussex, where I lived. From then on he became a frequent visitor to our home at Seven, Valencia Road, much to the annoyance of my rather austere father who considered him a bit of an upstart. Mother, on the other hand, was a kindly soul who took him at face value. And to my impish, eight-year-old sister Jacky, he was a sugar daddy who kept her well suppled with chocolate bars.

I liked having him around, but that's as far as it went. In the bloom of girlish youth, with my small neat figure and blond shoulder-length hair, I wasn't hard to look at and was never short of male companions, usually the local college boys.

Bill was decidedly different.

He was older, twenty-four to my nineteen years. And in his army uniform he was a smart and dapper escort. He had dark brown curly hair, soft brown eyes that twinkled kindly, and his upper lip sported a small moustache. None of the college boys had moustaches.

Bill had seen action in North Africa and Europe with his regiment, the British Columbia Dragoons. With the war nearing its end, he was waiting to be shipped back home.

When he talked, it was of things strange and alien, of the places he had been and the sights he had seen. The different way people lived and went about their daily tasks in his country defied even my vivid imagination. As far as I was concerned, he could have been a being from another planet.

My English upbringing had been sheltered, to say the least: I had been educated in a private convent school for young ladies. But when I met Bill, I began to perceive a new dimension to life. A sense of adventure assailed me, but I was not yet ready for the matrimonial plunge. Besides that, I had to contend with father's black looks. So, in time, Bill departed for Canada and I resumed my acquaintance with the old college crowd.

It might have ended there, but Bill kept his promise to write. In the months that followed our love blossomed and grew. One day a small parcel arrived and in it was a diamond engagement ring. He had wooed and won me through the mails. Just one obstacle remained—father.

I lacked the courage to face him with the news, so once again I relied on the written word. I left a letter on his bedside table and waited for the results. Faced with the awful truth, he agreed to let Bill come back. Then father would take it from there.

I honestly believe that father thought he wouldn't come back. But a few weeks later Bill rang the doorbell, and father's countenance took on a surprised look that lasted a long time. Bill and I married and prepared for the journey to Canada. Father, mother and Jacky came to West Worthing Station to see us off. To this day I have not set eyes on my father again, although we correspond regularly by mail. I remember that dear man's lost look as he stood on the platform and waved while the train carried us out of sight, on its way to Southampton and the *Aquitania*.

Leaving Home

The war brides may have been apprehensive about the enormity of their decision to marry Canadian servicemen, but they were determined to see it through. For many of them this meant a long wait in England for transport to Canada. While they petitioned MPs and Canada House in London in an attempt to expedite matters, their returned husbands were complaining to officials in Ottawa.

In a letter dated June 6, 1946, an Ottawa official described the situation. On one particular day, "they ganged up on us inasmuch as five called at one time. At least two of them had been drinking." The men reminded him that the Government of Canada had promised that servicemen's dependents would follow them on the next boat. "When they gang up like that anything can happen," the official concluded. "They certainly were peeved over what they term 'delays'."

Delays notwithstanding, between August 1944 and the end of January 1947, the Department of National Defence moved 61,334 dependents from Great Britain and northwest Europe. Of that number, 41,351 were Canadian servicemen's wives, 19,737 children, and 246 dependents of Canadian Firefighters and others.

Counting the 1,687 persons transported prior to August 1944, those still waiting to go over and later marriage and birth figures, the final total of Canadian Service dependents of World War II was to be more than 70,000 persons.

The task of transporting the war brides from England and the Continent was an enormous one. To handle the work, the Department of National Defence set up the Canadian Wives' Bureau which dealt not only with transportation but also information and welfare services. It was the first time in history that any government had provided home-to-home transportation for the dependents of its servicemen.

Moving troops in the war years had become commonplace, but transporting thousands of civilian women and their children was a different kind of problem. Available ships were refitted to deal with the unusual needs of the passengers. Regulations were drawn up covering luggage allowances (500 pounds for one to three dependents; 150 pounds for each additional dependent) and meal allowances (breakfast and lunch, seventy-five cents; dinner, one dollar). And special arrangements were made for accommodation and aid should any unforeseen problems arise.

The regulations made it clear that each dependent was entitled to one journey only, and that to be Canadian-bound. The war brides would not be given Canadian exit permits to return to Britain while the war continued. Should they succeed in returning by any other means, they would not become eligible for free transportation a second time.

On their way to an unknown land to be reunited with husbands they barely knew, the war brides were understandably nervous. Some panicked and seized this last chance to back out. But most carried on, sustained by the momentum of their adventure. At train stations and docks they embraced for the last time parents and relatives they might never see again, and as the ships pulled out of the harbour watched all that was familiar to them fade into the distance.

On board the converted luxury liners, troop and hospital ships that carried them across the Atlantic, they lived in a kind of limbo, occupying themselves with the demands of child-care and the delights of new friendships and newly-discovered shipboard food. Most of the women experienced seasickness, but at least that came to an end when the ships docked in Halifax. Homesickness didn't.

In the war brides' memories of that unforgettable Atlantic crossing, intense emotions dominate—excitement and anticipation mingling with a sharp nostalgia for the past and an anxiety toward a future they were on the verge of discovering.

The office of the Wives Bureau was located on Regent Street in London. It occupied the third floor of a fashionable and expensive store known as Galleries Lafayette.

The transportation of Canadian servicemen's wives and children to Canada was carried out from this office under a fairly complicated but ingenious system. In spite of headaches galore, I found the job fascinating and challenging.

We'd receive lists naming women and children from another department of the bureau, then a grouping of dependents had to be compiled and processed in time to coincide with the sailing schedules. Berthing accommodation had to be allocated according to the age and sex of children, and some wives had several. The breakdown of statistics may have seemed unnecessary to an outsider, but the complication of moving such a vast and varied crowd of people was no easy matter.

Girls from all over Britain and the Continent were transported to London and lodged in hostels until leaving for their ships. People on the hostel staff told me of occasional trouble: some women didn't care to be penned up or restricted; some of them would manage to sneak out for a night on the town. Of course, the staff had a definite responsibility for the wives—to see that they were well cared for and that nothing harmful happened to them. I realize that they were so many bodies to us, but we really tried to see the human beings behind all the statistics.

Through the strange workings of official bureaucracy we would pick up Scottish girls in Glasgow, hostel them in London and ship them from Southampton. In many cases the continental wives would come in through the southern ports, be hostelled in London and then trained up to Glasgow to sail from Scotland. I objected to the senselessness of the exercise and managed to get a few changes made. But

Photo by Captain Robinson. Public Archives of Canada.

Endless paper work faced the war brides before they could join their husbands in Canada. Here a Canadian Army sergeant helps a group of Dutch brides fill out transport application forms.

fighting the government was no easier in wartime than in peacetime and more often than not, I hit my head against a brick wall.

Naturally the girls were extremely interested in Canada, and hostel and train staff did their best to enlighten them. I could answer their questions about Nova Scotia and New Brunswick; other staff members would be knowledgeable about their respective areas of the country. We found that we had to correct and deglamorize many of the yarns they'd been spun.

One thing used to really annoy me—when a bride changed her mind after the ship was loaded. Suddenly she'd decide that she didn't know anything, or didn't want to know anything about Canada, and she was going home. Then she'd walk off the ship.

One woman in particular comes to mind. Three times she

changed her mind and walked down the gangplank. She had to be crossed off the nominal rolls; her three children had to be taken off; the totals on those sheets had to be changed; and the final totals all had to be changed. Every nominal roll, every copy had to be corrected—all while the liner waited.

I remember this same bride came once more to the office just prior to my departure for home. She was trying to get on yet another draft. I told her that as long as I was there, she'd never have a chance.

However, I *can* understand a certain amount of reluctance on the part of wives. It was a formidable step to leave home for a country about which they knew practically nothing. In lots of cases what little they did know was incorrect, fed to them by romanticizing young men. But three times down the gangplank holding up the ships, that was enough!

After each draft was processed, we'd stand on the docks watching the hundreds of young women and children embark. There was a great sense of relief when they were all on the ship. But sadness was in the air, too, as the girls left their native lands. To an interested observer the courage and trust of those young women was touching. Each one was going thousands of miles from home and family on the word of a guy she really didn't know too well.

I can still see a cluster of Parisienne ladies in their short skirts and sophisticated make-up. They looked like a troupe of chorus girls, and I couldn't help wondering where in Canada they'd be settling. How would they fit in on the prairies, in the backwoods, or as fishermen's wives?

Rev. L. H. Sutcliffe was formerly with the Canadian Army Corps of Military Staff Clerks.

It was August 1946 when I received my documents allowing me to leave Wales for Canada. At last, that very special envelope with my boat ticket and visa.

I well remember the look on my mother's face. And the heartbreak and excitement at the same time for me. I told my mother, "Don't worry, I'll be home in six months. I'll talk Alf into coming back to Wales with me."

We had to stay in London overnight, and I know a couple of war brides who went back home from the hostel. We were all so homesick that night in London and only the thoughts of seeing husbands and our new country kept the rest of us going.

When I got word to leave for Canada it was all very hush hush. I wasn't allowed to tell my family the name of the port of embarkation or the ship. My relatives all came to the station to say goodbyes to me and my one-year-old daughter. About a hundred war brides boarded the train along with soldier escorts and were locked in. As the train pulled out of Glasgow, one girl began singing "Bonnie Scotland I Adore Thee". That opened up the flood gates, and most of us cried until we were well out of the city.

I remember the underground train journey to the check-in depot vividly. My brother, who had recently returned from four years war service in the Middle East, went with me. How hard it was to fight back the tears and thoughts such as, I'll never do this again.

At the depot in London I met another young bride who was very expectant and very tearful. We set out to cheer each other up.

My parents came to Waterloo Station, London, and saw me put aboard a special war brides bus. We all thought we were going straight over to Euston Station, but we ended up in a big house in Park Lane. The boat hadn't arrived at Liverpool.

The house had belonged to some titled man, and there were raves in the papers about the wonderful marble staircase. We certainly didn't think it was wonderful; we cursed it every time we had to toil up and down, frightened that our little ones might slip and land at the bottom.

The food was awful, so we went to Marks in Oxford Street and filled up. We had to sign in and out—I suppose they were afraid of losing us.

I phoned my mother who thought I was already at sea. I could easily have popped back to Chiswick on the tube, but no way did I want to go through a second set of goodbyes.

I felt somewhat guilty about leaving England before the war was over. I was advised to report to London on May 5, 1945, and had no idea that the European phase of the war would end that day.

It was no big wrench for me to leave my family as I'd hardly ever lived with them, except for holidays. As a child I'd gone to boarding school, and because my father was a career army officer my parents were abroad a great deal.

As for going to a strange country—I felt excited, as if I were an explorer, but I realized the risk involved. A sermon I had heard a few weeks prior to leaving England gave me courage. The minister preached about Naomi and Ruth and quoted Ruth saying: "For whither thou goest, I will go; and where thou lodgest, I will lodge; thy people shall be my people and thy God my God." That really impressed me and many times later, if I felt depressed in Canada or wanted to return to England, I'd repeat that verse to myself. I felt that I had to go to Canada, become a Canadian and adapt to the Canadian way of living.

We were not told that the war had ended until late in the evening. We could hear a big commotion going on outside, but nobody would tell us what was going on. We were not allowed near a telephone, and VE Day was nearly over when we went out to board buses that night. The buses took us to "an unnamed station" where we took trains to an "unnamed destination" (Liverpool). Early the next morning we embarked for Canada on the *Duchess of Bedford*.

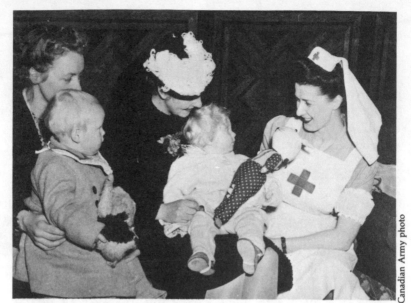

Canadian Army photo

Wives and families of Canadian servicemen gathered at the Maple Leaf service club awaiting transport to Canada.

The *Aquitania* looked like a great white mansion as our train drew alongside that sunny April day at Southampton. As she slowly eased away from the dock a Salvation Army Band was playing "Wish Me Luck As You Wave Me Good-bye" and "Aulde Lang Syne". When I saw my native land disappearing, I had the strongest urge to jump overboard and swim back. I had to grip the rail and force myself not to do it. Other war brides on the ship confessed to the same sensation. Leaving one's country might be compared to losing an arm or leg: until severing actually happens, one can't imagine the strength of the bond or the terrifying wrench of separation.

WAR BRIDES—JANUARY 1947
by Gwyneth M. Shirley

Southampton harbour in the gloom
Of a rainswept, winter day;
The shouts of stevedores, sliding ropes
And a troopship, hulking, grey.

Two solitary bobbies pace
The damp deserted dock.
A sweeping seagull screams farewell,
The echo seems to mock.

A Royal Navy band appears,
Black oilskins shine in the rain.
A harsh discordant clash of sound
Expresses their disdain.

"Our own lads were not good enough,
Neither Tom, Dick nor Harry.
So 'Rule Brittania' loud and clear,
For here we will not tarry."

The Aquitania slowly shifts
Her great bulk, sirens sound,
A shrill salute to this old ship
On her last voyage bound.

Six hundred war brides crowd on deck
To watch the fading shore,
And wartime years "blood, sweat and tears"
Flood deep the memory's core.

Rain pitted water, smoking stacks,
The land — a ribbon thin.
"Oh, can we hope to see again
Our country and our kin?"

Twice in a lifetime this old ship
Took men across the sea.
Wars pass away but love survives
To win the Victory.

Reprinted with permission of *Legion Magazine*.

I remember how blithely I set out on that big adventure, thinking that I could pop back to England for a visit. Canada really wasn't all that far away, I reasoned.

Then, as just another war bride among the hundreds, I spent the first night billetted in Park Lane, London. It was the only time I had ever stayed at such an exotic address. The next morning we were transported by bus to Waterloo Station, taking a last look at Big Ben as we drove by. I remember wondering how life could go on as usual when there we were, a busload of girls, starting out on a traumatic journey.

And so down to Southampton and aboard the old *Aquitania*. My first time on a liner was not what I'd expected. All the state rooms had disappeared and we were herded, about fifty at a time, to sleep in bunks behind sheets of canvas. There were hundreds of girls, but one in particular remains in my mind. Behind our canvas room was another sleeping area, and there seemed to be all Scots girls there. I never met them, but one seemed to be the life of their party. Her name was Sadie. Sadie from Glasgow, wherever you are, I remember you and have wondered through the years where you went and how life treated you.

Under those strange conditions we enjoyed the gorgeous food—white bread and fresh fruit especially—and I'm sure we were all gluttons. Everyone was kind and helpful. Laundry and washrooms were filled to overflowing with baby nappies and other washing. I was so glad to be a "single wife"—that is, one without children. I still admire those women who set out on that journey with little ones. The pioneer spirit was still very much alive in the war brides.

Len was injured while on training in Scotland and spent quite a while in hospital in England before he was discharged and sent home to Canada. I was looking forward to joining him, but by that time I was pregnant with our second child and wasn't allowed to join him until the baby was five months old and Len had found an apartment. We

Cunard White Star   *Scythia*

wrote every week and eventually word came that he had found a place to live and I was to report to a hostel in London to await sailing orders. I had about three weeks to pack.

We weren't able to leave the hostel once we got there or communicate with anyone; there was still danger of being torpedoed. When orders finally came through, we were put on the train for Southampton.

I arrived at the dock with a two year old by the hand, a baby in my arms, diapers, formula and all the other things you need when travelling with a baby. I looked up at the *Queen Mary*—it was enormous and there was a gangplank leading up to it. There was no way I could make it up that gangplank, and I knew it. I don't usually cry, but I did that day, just stood there and wept. Two soldiers came down from the ship and helped me. If they hadn't, I don't know what I'd have done.

We got on board and there were streamers and the band was playing "Will Ye No Come Back Again". And then the ship started to inch out, and the streamers started to snap and that was just the most awful feeling. I just felt, that was it.

As the *Lady Nelson* prepared to leave Southampton, war brides and returning servicemen lined the dock.

We were kept pretty busy on board ship looking after the children and making sure they were fed and clean. But when we were about half way across the Atlantic, I began to wonder if I had done the right thing. I wondered if Len still loved me and if I still loved him. It was a terrible feeling. I really didn't know what to expect.

Two days before my scheduled departure for Canada, my husband arrived back in England. He'd spent nearly two years fighting in Italy and northwest Europe and would have to rejoin his regiment in Holland. We went to Canada House in London to see if my passage could be postponed, so that I could spend the leave with him. Despite disappointment and tears, I took the advice of the authorities there to go as planned.'Otherwise I might have had to wait until most of the servicemen were taken home and the end of the war was anticipated.

At sea, brides "without children" made friends, enjoyed the food and tried to stave off seasickness.

I believe it was March 26, 1945 when I left Reigate. We arrived at the London hostel to the wail of an air raid siren and later learned that V2 rockets had landed near the docks.

Next morning we were on a train for Liverpool, where we waited while three shiploads of war brides and returning servicemen were collected together. The family of one Liverpool girl would come onto the quay each day before we left and wave and wave to her. Sooner or later the poor girl would break down and run to her cabin and sob her heart out. Another woman spotted her husband coming aboard. She was astounded—and so was he—and she flew into his arms.

When we finally set sail in convoy, it was Easter weekend, and the mothers had run out of baby food. They'd been instructed to take along enough to last the babies seven days. Several babies were sick from the substitute food provided on board, and some of the mothers fell ill from seasickness. We women without children helped out.

There was no entertainment of any kind on our ship. On deck were only a few wooden benches, and we had to use our lifejackets as cushions on the floor if we wished to sit outside. It was hot and stuffy down below where the cabins and lounge were: with the ship blacked out, no air came through the portholes. The husband mentioned earlier remarked dryly, "A lovely way to spend a honeymoon!"

Just weeks after we were married my RCAF husband was posted to India. He was there three years. Then came the wonderful news that he was returning to Canada for repatriation, via England. Could I get my discharge from the WAAF and go with him? After delays, red tape and a great deal of help from the Canadian government, in May 1945 I was at last bording a ship bound for Canada.

The greatest thrill came as I walked up the gangplank. "Hi, Eleanor," a familiar voice called, and there on the deck was my husband, Wyn. We had no idea we'd be on the same ship. Fate or the authorities had been good to us. We sailed on the ex-cruise ship, the *Athlone Castle*.

All the war brides travelled in the old first-class quarters. Those with children were assigned to cabins; those without occupied bunk beds which were in tiers of four. I felt sorry for them because those in the upper three bunks had to stand on the lower one in order to climb aloft, and then if someone was seasick up there. . . .

We were allowed to meet our husbands at designated times and places. I remember saying how good the chicken had been at dinner and my husband saying, "What chicken?" Then we realized that our food was very different from that which was served to the troops on board. Some of us were in tears at our first meal and the sight of all that food. Oh, the white bread, bowls full of sugar, plates of butter, bacon and eggs for breakfast every morning and lovely fruit. It was like a dream. Only days before, at the reception centre in Liverpool, no food provision had been made for the toddlers. We wives without children had donated some of our bread and sausages so that the mothers wouldn't go without. And then suddenly, on the ship there was plenty of everything. After years of rationing and shortages, no wonder we wept.

Each morning we were woken up with tea brought by a stewardess. It went down very well indeed on those chilly mornings, and whenever I drink tea with canned milk in it, I always think of those mornings on the bride ship.

I sailed to Canada on the *Scythia*, a Cunard-White Star liner. I'd never even been in a row boat before, let alone a near 20,000-ton job.

We war brides had gone through many tearful sessions at home when the enormity of the step we were taking finally hit us. Then there were more tears and lumps in throats as the *Scythia* left Liverpool to quayside bands playing "Will Ye No Come Back Again" and "Aulde Lang Syne".

The *Scythia* was in for mechanical trouble and rough seas.

Part of her story was reported in the *Daily Mail*, February 22, 1946, by James A. Robinson:

A feverish race to repair the crippled Cunard-White Star liner *Scythia* (19,761 tons), which is wallowing in heavy seas at the mouth of Belfast Lough with 500 Canadian servicemen's brides and 300 children on board, is now in progress to get her under way again for Halifax.

Gear which was rushed from Liverpool to Belfast, following a radio message from the liner to the Cunard-White Star head office in Liverpool was put on board the *Scythia* today.

A gang of workmen from Harland and Wolff's will remain in the liner until repairs are completed.

Captain Bateman, the commander, radioed exact details of what was required when the liner developed turbo-feed trouble less than twenty-four hours after leaving Liverpool.

This mishap is a blow to the Canadian war brides. They had taken a tearful farewell of Britain on Tuesday but had recovered their spirits as they got out to sea—only to be plunged into a fresh bout of homesickness as they saw the green fields of Ireland from the liner today.

A trifle sad and bewildered, they are wondering when they will see the land where their husbands are waiting.

Strenuous efforts are being made to get the *Scythia* ready to resume her voyage tomorrow, but she may not be able to sail before Saturday.

Three hundred tons of fresh water, 200 gallons of milk and many tons of fresh fish are being put aboard tomorrow, for the mishap has dislocated the catering.

The milk is primarily for the 251 children and 41 infants on board.

I recall that one ailing expectant mother was taken off on a stretcher at Belfast. The rest of us clubbed around while the ship was being repaired to raise money to pay her air fare to Canada.

Once underway, the voyage was storm-tossed and the Atlantic air bitterly cold. During the worst of the weather and seasickness, I thought that I must have been mad to have left dry land. I was jolly glad to see Halifax.

Brides "with children"
occupied their time
running after active
children, supervising meals
and washing diapers in the
ships' cramped quarters.
By 1946 more than 21,000
children had been
transported to Canada.

I sailed for Canada on June 19, 1946. I was expecting my first child and was so seasick that I thought I'd lose the baby. On the whole, the nurses on board seemed very cold towards the war brides, although they were good to me. I saw some girls so ill that they couldn't lift their heads from pillows. They were never visited or checked by a doctor. One nurse who came round advised them to get up on deck. I've often thought that I should like to have been at that one's beside when she went into labour with her first child. . . .

The war brides stuck it out together and helped each other. If one of them was well enough to go for a meal she would bring back fruit or something light for others to eat. Then, if they were sick again, they'd at least have something to bring up.

Living not far from the port of Southampton as I did, it seemed rather foolish of the authorities to send me all the way up to Liverpool to embark. My sister came part way with me, but it was a sad day. As we made our farewells, I did not expect to see her again. Besides that, I had always enjoyed the beauties which belonged to the English countryside alone. I had a deep attachment to my church, interests in good music, drama and swimming. And I knew I was leaving it all behind. Not ignorant of the topographical regions of Canada, I knew that only on Vancouver Island would I find similar conditions to those in England. But alas! I was going to the vast open spaces of Saskatchewan where the winters were long and hard. I was somewhat apprehensive.

The army provided excellent transportation for us, even if the cabins were a mite overcrowded—six adults and six children to a cabin. It was suggested that war brides without children should help those with, should the need arise. In my case it didn't work out. The girls in my cabin had friends from their neighbourhoods in other parts of the ship, so I was left alone to cope with a very healthy and active little boy, while I suffered from seasickness from the first day out. What should have been an interesting and exciting experience turned out to be a living nightmare. Only those who have known the misery of seasickness will fully understand the extent of my plight.

The meals supplied were excellent for we had use of the officers' mess. Yet the very smell of food, combined with that of fresh paint and oil from the engines and the excessive heat, made it impossible for me to eat anything but a few soda crackers. I remember one steward laughing at me as I was being pulled towards the dining room by my small son. My reluctance was noticeable!

At Halifax we were welcomed by a brass band and newspaper reporters. I recall one woman pushing to the fore. She was determined that she and her five children would be photographed for posterity. From somewhere in the crowd I heard the comment, "Good Lord, some soldier must have married her the first day he landed in England!" As we disembarked we were met by army personnel, one man to each suitcase and child. They escorted us to our allotted seats on the train. I have high praise for the way the Canadian Army attended to our every comfort.

Late in August 1942 I was told to report to Canada House, "as someone has taken an interest in your case". I promptly made the journey to London and was instructed to go for an American visa the following day. I protested that I must keep appointments at my work, then sat stunned at the reply: "Such appointments can hardly be important if you are sailing for Canada on Saturday." Saturday was only three days away! It was explained that five months pregnancy was the limit allowed for such voyages, but an exception was being made in my case.

My passport was stamped "wife of a government official"; my ticket was made out first class. I never knew for certain how all this came about. I was only concerned with trying to pack (that lovely baby pram had to be returned to the shop) and to get to Scotland within two days.

On arrival a bedraggled group of us wandered around the village of Gourock all day in the rain, while our ship waited for us in Greenock, or was it the other way around?

First class turned out to be an interior cabin with four bunks and no fresh air. It was to hold three adults, two teenage girls and little twin boys of three. The latter had to sleep away from their mother in the men's quarters but spent the rest of their time with us.

The passengers on our deck seemed to be mostly Canadian and American wives returning home. Woe betide any of us who dared say hello to the army or navy personnel on the deck below! There was to be no fraternization, even between the many married couples.

We ate at different times and passed the men on our way out of the dining room. We had to negotiate a narrow gangway where the servicemen were lined up for the next call for breakfast. The rolling of the ship, my awkward shape and occupied hands caused me to collide with every fifth man as I bounced off the wall. Willing hands assisted me and encouraging voices called, "Watch it, mother, careful!" I was probably the only woman on board who touched those forbidden men.

Our ship, the *Monterey*, was on loan from the American government, crew and food included. Imagine the reactions of a pregnant woman, accustomed to wartime rations and having spent a night in a stuffy, crowded cabin when faced with so much food. The menu included fruit or fruit juice, hot or cold cereal, two eggs and five slices of bacon, pancakes with syrup, toast with jam, cinnamon buns and fresh fruit. This substantial meal was supposed to sustain us until supper time. I would just look bleakly at the steward, request a lemon and say, "Please, could I have a bowl of fruit for my cabin." Each noon I lined up with the children on board for crackers and milk, the only alternative to O Henry bars and other such confections so foreign to our taste.

I married an officer in the Royal Canadian Engineers and was working as a speech pathologist in the brain injuries unit at Bangour Hospital, near Edinburgh. We had met at the beginning of the war in London, where I was completing my training. Whilst in Edinburgh, at a neuro-surgical convention, I met the commanding officer of the Canadian Neurological Hospital at Basingstoke, who told me that the Department of Health and Pensions (or DVA as it is now called) was anxious to start a speech treatment centre for the brain-injured Canadian servicemen at Christie Street Hospital in Toronto. They asked me if I would be interested. As my husband was serving on the Italian front with the First Canadian Division, I agreed to precede him to Canada.

Because it was wartime, all details concerning our departure and destination were top secret. The baggage labels with which I was supplied bore just my name, priority number (due to the urgent need of my services in Toronto I had been given priority over all other brides proceeding to Canada) and the coded numbers of our port and destination.

It was the end of September 1944 when I was instructed to report to an address on St. James Street, London at 10:00 p.m. It was pitch dark, black as only a moonless night in the blackout could be. Many girls, children and relatives were gathered together in the big room, and several were in tears. Around midnight we were divided into two groups, "brides with" and "brides without children". The classification lasted throughout the trip. Fortunately, I fell into the latter category.

We were loaded on to buses and taken through the dark streets to St. Pancras Station which I think was cordoned off. A train was waiting for us, and many Red Cross workers were there to assist the mothers and children. The train was under military control and sundry cheery soldiers kept popping their heads into our compartment to see if we were all right, waking us up in the process.

We had no idea whether we were headed for Liverpool or a Clydeside port, but in the grey light of morning we arrived alongside a jetty in Liverpool. The camouflaged liner berthed there turned out to be the old *Mauritania*. It was under the control of the RCAF.

I was assigned to what had originally been a two-berth cabin which now contained three or four two-tiered bunks. There was no room to do anything else but stand on a narrow strip of floor or lie flat on one's bunk. In fact, as I recall, the only place in the whole ship where one could sit down in a chair was in the dining room. The salons and lounges were full of bunks and hammocks for the countless servicemen being transported back and forth across the Atlantic.

We followed quite a southerly route and enjoyed sunny, warm days. Twenty-four hours before we were due to arrive at Halifax, a flying boat came out and signalled the ship. It turned out that a freighter had been sunk off Halifax harbour, and we were to delay our arrival by twenty-four hours. We spent that time zig-zagging around, and all Service personnel on board were placed on submarine watch.

We finally reached Halifax at 6:00 a.m. on Saturday morning of Thanksgiving weekend. The ship's turn around was so fast that immediately after we tied up the crew started taking supplies on board for the return voyage, and airmen embarked on their way to the war zone.

We had to vacate the cabins immediately. Once again, except for mealtimes, there was nowhere to sit. And it was pouring with rain. As we tied up at the pier, we were temporarily cheered by a military band playing from one of the sheds. But after a while even they seemed to get discouraged and left the scene.

I shall never forget the humour in the sight of a group of disconsolate brides sitting on a pile of mail bags. The mail bags carried the sign, OUT OF BOUNDS TO ALL RANKS.

I crossed on the *Aquitania* which had been used as a troop ship and prisoner-of-war carrier. The war brides had the old first-class quarters and were carefully guarded from the thousand-plus returning servicemen on lower decks. With a good number of others, I had a berth in what once had been the stewards' mess. There were some washrooms on our deck enclosed in barbed wire cages and flapping canvas — very chilly!

One day, some girls told me that they were frightened of a woman who kept falling about and acting strangely. I investigated and then got in touch with the ship's doctor. The girl was placed in hospital. Late on the last night of the voyage, I was called to the sick bay and asked to sign her release, get her papers checked, explain Canadian money to her and generally be responsible. She was bound for the Prairies.

I had been informed that she had meningitis and warned that it wasn't to be revealed or the ship would be held up. It was intimated that she had to walk off the ship, and I had to deliver her to the Red Cross. I agreed to see it through. Two youthful soldiers followed us, carrying our suitcases, while I supported the unfortunate girl.

During the war I was in the Auxiliary Territorial Service stationed at Wellington Barracks, London. London was also my home.

My RCAF husband of nine months was posted back to Canada, and I was given a compassionate discharge in order to go with him. However, due to foul-ups, Bob left before I did. I finally received my sailing orders in January 1945.

Our draft, about 120 war brides and 35 children, left from Greenock, Scotland. Our designated ship, the *Louis Pasteur*, had developed engine trouble and we boarded a freighter. Before the war the *Mataroa* had been on a South African run. We joined a convoy of more than 200 ships, which took three or four days to get into position.

For some children, the crossing was a bewildering experience. For others, the ships were floating amusement parks.

The girls travelling without children were in cabins normally for two persons, but a third bunk had been slipped in between the original two. The women with children were in larger rooms. Babies and children slept in cribs or in hammocks slung beside the mother's bunk.

We were not allowed to close our cabin doors, which were hooked open to prevent jamming. This was in case we were hit by an enemy torpedo. We carried our lifejackets with us everywhere and took part in daily lifeboat drills. Sometimes there was a drill in the middle of the night. We were instructed not to get completely undressed and to keep warm clothes nearby at all times.

The weather got progressively worse. At one point we were battened down for three days and only the crew was permitted on deck.

I was one of the lucky half dozen or so war brides who were not seasick. We few looked after the babies who were

Photo by Lt. I. Iewan. Canadian Army photo. Public Archives of Canada.

also free of seasickness. It was a nightmare, and we didn't have a doctor on board. Medication and instructions were received from another ship in the convoy.

We did a lot of zig-zagging to confuse U-boats and went as far south as the Azores. The weather improved and the girls gained their sea-legs. Then the babies started getting sick with diarrhea and vomiting. We were also running short of baby food.

There were some musical people on board and we enjoyed concert parties, amateur nights and charades. The war brides exchanged addresses, played cards, cried, laughed and altogether became one large family.

After twenty-one days at sea, the sight of land produced strange sensations. We had been through so much together and had so much yet to face.

Sadness and joy were all mixed together for us at Halifax. Ambulances waited to take fifteen very sick children to hospital, and I remember vividly that three girls were informed that their husbands had been killed in Europe while we had been crossing the Atlantic.

I must say I feel like chuckling every time I hear the term "war brides". Three-quarters of the girls on board were pregnant, and most had a child or two in tow as well.

We must have looked a pretty sight, lining the rails, when we sailed into Halifax, scared, tired, homesick and rounded. On the pier was a band to welcome us, playing, you guessed it, "Here Comes the Bride". That really broke us up and the laughter did us good.

We arrived in Halifax on March 2, 1946. A band and dignitaries were there to greet us. People were throwing streamers, oranges, bananas and money. It was very exciting.

A friend has told me about the music played by the band when her ship docked, "Nights of Gladness". Rather appropriate, since servicemen and wives had been apart so much.

When I left Bournemouth to go to Liverpool, I was a frightened nineteen-year-old girl. My husband had left six months previously for his home on Prince Edward Island. I sailed from Liverpool on September 30, 1946, aboard the Letitia. When we landed at Halifax on October 8, the ship's name had been changed to Empire Brent.

About all I can remember about the voyage is that I helped out girls who were sick and cared for some of the little children. And that some kind soul stole my green coat which I needed so badly when I arrived in Canada. I had left home in summer clothing, and in Halifax it was cold and windy.

Some of the girls promised to keep in touch, but of course they never did. I wonder what happened to them. I hope their lives turned out better than mine. If I had known what was ahead of me, I would never have left England.

. . . Canada is just ahead. To most of you it ushers in the advent of a new life with new adventures and responsibilities, the success or failure of which depends on the stability and determination of each individual. I am absolutely confident that you will not only be worthy of the confidence and trust imposed in you by Canada's fighting men, but that you will be citizens that Canada may be justly proud of.

There awaits you in the sheltered harbour of Halifax a welcome the warmth of which will extend from one end of the Dominion to the other. Canada welcomes you with a deep feeling of pride—you who are truly representative of the remarkable womanhood of Britain, who during the long dark years of war, stood so courageously, who sacrificed so bravely, and who contributed so materially to the magnificent war effort—all of which won the deep admiration of all decent peoples of the world.

British stock such as this is indeed a welcome addition to our country; and your lovely children, the likes of which I have never seen surpassed, should grow up under Canada's sunny skies, true stalwarts of parents who have proven their worth as real men and women—and on their shoulders will rest the future responsibility of guiding the National Affairs of State and the future destiny of Canada.

Going through the Nurseries on the Ship and looking into the faces of these lovely children, I so often think of the quotation read by Prime Minister Mackenzie King, in giving his fine talk to all on board last Voyage when he read—quote—"The tiniest bits of opinion sown in the minds of children in private life afterwards issue forth to the world and become public opinion; for Nations are gathered out of Nurseries, and they who hold the leading strings of children may even exercise a greater power than those who hold the reins of Government. . . . "

Lieutenant-Colonel W. E. Sutherland, OBE, commandant of the *Queen Mary* on her last voyage as a troop ship.

I served with the RCAF (Women's Division) during World War II and for a time worked at the Canadian Wives Bureau in London, England. There we typed lists of names for each ship load going to Canada, sent letters out to the war brides with accompanying information packets, luggage labels and so on. I often wish that I had made copies of some of the letters received. I remember one wanting to bring her piano to Canada. Others would write who had no intention of ever going to Canada and tell us what we could do with their tickets. Then a week later there'd be requests for passage on the next boat.

I returned to Canada in October 1946 aboard the *Aquitania*. There were 1500 war brides on that ship, mostly Dutch. Our accommodations were very poor, and we were crowded together in the hold of the ship. There were canvas separations and eight to ten of us to each so-called cabin. Some of the Dutch girls were next door, and we got acquainted with them. Some could speak English well, others not at all. They told us some very sad stories of their ordeals at the hands of the Germans during the war, how they were starved and had to resort to eating tulip bulbs at times. They told of having anything of value taken from them including their clothes and how, after liberation, they made clothes from blankets and shirts given to them by Canadian soldiers.

I felt very sorry for those girls. I was glad to get off the boat in Halifax with only a short distance to go from there to my home near Parrsboro, N.S. I thought of some of them going all the way across Canada on crowded trains to an unknown destination. I wondered what fate awaited them.

Holly L. Spicer.

A few miles out of Halifax the *Queen Mary* ran into dense fog. There we were, enveloped in the warm, heavy mist with radar spinning, fog horns blowing and ships' bells ringing frequently.

On August 11, 1946, the Captain decided to allow tugs to ease the huge liner into port. The *Queen Mary* became a fairyland of lights, and the inhabitants of Halifax lit up their town to reciprocate. When the fog lifted, we saw giant banners of greeting. "Welcome to Our War Brides," they said, and wished the settlers happiness in their new land.

Special well-marked trains stood by, ready to take the immigrants to their final destinations.

Newspaper reporters had a field day as they flocked on board taking pictures and interviewing war brides. The disembarkation took two days. Besides the human cargo there was a large number of prams, cots and innumerable pieces of luggage to be unloaded and then reloaded onto the trains.

We felt sorry to part company with the war brides; it was like losing good friends and something precious. It was sad to see all those lovely babies go, lost to Britain and her post-war needs.

I should like to have gone with each young woman to see where she'd live, how she was welcomed and whether her pre-conceived ideas matched reality. I trust a happy life was in store for most. What qualms and thrills they must have experienced as they settled into a new life.

Mrs. Beatrice E. Caton was a private passenger on the *Queen Mary* on one of the war bride crossings.

Autographs

Catherine Hind.

M. F. Pollock

Leslie Williams

Frederick E. E. Davis

F. Harris.

Kay Owens

Kathleen Phair.

Edith Ponts.

G. Goldsmith

Connie Henderson.

Mary Pajukiewicz

Lilian Looby

R. C. Murray. C.O

R. Downey

H. R. Robson

Shelley Cotman

Wishing we had some Lemonade!
Peggy Ennis & Chris
Vanduta Sask
Canada.

J. H. Johnson.

H. Fraser.

R.M.S. "SCYTHIA"   28th February, 1946

Diner d'Adieu

MENU

Petite Marmite

Fillets of Sole—Meuniere

Roast Chicken with Bread Sauce

Buttered Green Peas

Boiled and Browned Potatoes

Plum Pudding—Brandy Sauce

Fresh Fruit

Coffee

When we sailed into Halifax the sight was hard to describe. The weather was such that there was a fairy mist, and we could only see parts of objects, portions of other vessels, a dismembered tree afloat, glimpses of land, and all appeared to be floating in a rosy, misty glow. It was exquisitely beautiful and unforgettable.

Suddenly the ethereal mist gave way to the quay and people waving and cheering and the usual bustle that accompanies the arrival of an ocean liner. It dawned on me that all that water lay between me and England—and I still had a long way to go.

Canada—First Impressions

It was a beautiful sight, that June day, with the fog lifting gently, like the curtain going up on a play. The scene was Halifax harbour.

As the war brides stepped off the ships, they were met by Red Cross personnel who put them on special trains that were waiting to take them to destinations across the country. The Red Cross made every possible effort to notify the women's husbands or in-laws of their arrival and tried, in a myriad of small ways, to make the transition smoother.

But Canada was not home, and the war brides soon noticed the differences. The abundance of food, the vastness of the country and the friendliness of the people—these were things which immediately impressed them. But as they left the brides trains and began new lives, they became aware of the enormous social and cultural adjustments required of them.

At cities and towns across the country, the women lined the windows of the trains to watch reunions of departing brides and their Canadian husbands. Some were warmly received and quickly drawn into a supportive family circle. Others were less fortunate. The romantic fantasies of life in Canada created in forgetfulness and longing by soldier husbands far from home were often shattered by a cruel reality.

In the following excerpts, the war brides recall those first few traumatic days and weeks in Canada, and observers—Red Cross officials and volunteers—document some of the tragic endings to stories which began with such hopeful expectations in Halifax.

Dear Fellow Canadians:

We have no PA system so we are taking this means of advising you on matters which we are sure will prove useful to you.

DON'T Send telegrams without first referring the details to a Train Liaison Officer. We appreciate you are anxious to advise your husband, etc. about arrival times, but this is unnecessary as he or they have been told by the Canadian authorities the time and place to meet you. Our experience has shown that wires giving times of arrival have frequently caused confusion and upsets in well laid plans. If you must send a wire, speak to the Train Liaison Officer first.

DON'T Use the occasional stops of the train for shopping purposes. Unfortunately we have found that the girls at stops have gone into the town's shopping areas. You are not familiar with Canadian money or Canadian prices and it is more than just a possibility that you may make a mistake which you will not be able to detect. Shop in your new home town.

DON'T Give money to strangers at stops in order that they may purchase something for you. Speak to the Officers on the train about your needs.

DON'T Over tip. If you don't understand the money value, ask any of the Train Staff.

DON'T Stray too far from the train when it stops when you are permitted to get off. You may be left behind.

DO Be careful at mealtime. Rich foods, lack of exercise and long rail journeys especially in the summer months cause many minor complaints.

DO Make certain you understand the route letter you secure when you move independently to another train.

DO Try to keep your accommodation area neat and washrooms clean, please.

DO Keep your handbag with you at all times as tickets must be checked at intervals on the trip.

DO Consult the Doctor, Canadian Red Cross VAD nurse if you or your child feel ill.

DO Refer any problems concerning money, transfer of funds etc. you have to the Train Liaison Officer whose only interest is your well-being.

DO Send air mail letters to relatives in the U.K. instead of costly cables. Air mail will give seven days service and CRX will supply Air Mail forms.

If you desire to show your appreciation to the CRX or other voluntary organizations for their services, join one of them in your own home town.

Issued by Department of National Defence, Ottawa, Ontario.

I met about thirty-five war brides while I was president of the Sackville, N.B. branch of the Canadian Red Cross Society. In the majority of cases everything went off as planned. I'd receive a telephone call from the Red Cross in Moncton informing me that Mrs. So-and-So would arrive on a certain train that evening. Then I'd go in search of her husband, and we'd meet the train and hubby would take his bride away with him.

But there were ball-ups at times. The worst I think concerned a young chap from Ottawa. He'd returned from Europe, landed in Montreal, then home to Ottawa where his family decided to motor to P.E.I., intending to pick up his bride at Sackville on the way. She had been on a slower ship and landed in Halifax. We got in touch with the commandant of her train, informing him that she should detrain at Sackville instead of going on to Ottawa. The train came in at 12:15 a.m. but didn't stop. Her husband and in-laws were left standing on the platform.

Canadian Army photo.

Like the other war brides, these women, arriving in Halifax on the converted *Mauritania* in February 1946, were the focus of considerable attention both in the press and among the Canadian people generally.

I immediately phoned the Red Cross in Moncton and asked them to hold the train. Meanwhile the husband and I jumped into my car and raced the twenty-eight miles to Moncton where we found Mrs. So-and-So would not get off the train because she was sure that her husband awaited her in Ottawa, not Sackville. Eventually we got permission to board the train, re-united hubby and wife, gathered up her belongings, got off the train and allowed it to proceed on its way.

The Moncton Branch of the Red Cross put the couple up at a hotel for the night. Later that morning the in-laws drove back to Moncton, picked up their son and daughter-in-law and journeyed on to P.E.I., while I tried to settle down again to my job in the bank.

Another comical one was the case of a bride coming from Halifax on the old Maritime Express. She was ticketed to detrain at Aulac, about four miles before Sackville. But that

Canadian Army photo.

Canadian Red Cross personnel were waiting to help mothers and their children disembark from the ships and board the special brides trains which were to take them to their new homes.

train did not stop at Aulac. We knew this and were waiting at Sackville station. Meanwhile, the conductor, thinking that we'd be at Aulac, transferred the bride to the eastbound Maritime Express which was about to pull out on the adjoining track. By the time we found out about all of this, our bride was on her way back to Aulac. Once again I jumped into my car and, after breaking all speed limits, arrived at Aulac just as our bride was stepping off the train. As I was the only person in sight, it was just as well that I was wearing my Red Cross armband and was able to convince her that her husband was on the way over in a slower motor car. After being rushed from one train to another, then alighting in the middle of fields with not a house in sight, only one person there and that person not her husband, who could have blamed her if for a short while, she wished that she were safely back in the Old Country.

Mr. J. R. Curry.

Two days out of New York, the *Wakefield* (peacetime *Mauritania*, I believe) caught fire and was left behind with destroyers. Rumour had it that there were servicemen only aboard and that the fire had been controlled. It was years before I heard that there had been no loss of life and that the ship was soon back in service.

At six o'clock on the morning of September 11, we awoke to find that we had arrived in New York. After breakfast we all disembarked to sit on our luggage in the huge baggage shed. By lunch time we were told to return to the ship for a meal. We heard that the Red Cross had offered to help us get to the railway station but had been told that such help was not needed. Later on frantic attempts were made to get the Red Cross to round up vehicles for us.

The ten pounds that we had been allowed to take out of England had been spent on tips and chocolate bars. Few of us could afford to pay the taxi drivers who offered to take us to the ferry. At least we knew that we were on an island and that walking was out of the question!

Back on the ship, I'd done my packing. Dressed in an English wool dress I became ill from the high temperature which had reached ninety degrees. The ship's doctor was sent for, and I was given a tranquilizer and told to sleep. Some hours later, I awoke to find myself alone with no idea how to get off the ship. Up and down the elevators I went looking for the gangplank, until I finally rejoined the passengers who were still waiting in the baggage shed.

At about 6:00 p.m. one vehicle arrived. It looked suspiciously like a Black Maria, with only two tiny windows at the rear, but we crowded around it eagerly. A very shy young man was asking that only women with babies take the seats. Seeing one seat still vacant, I stepped forward saying, "Please, I'm going to have one so may I have a seat?" He was so embarrassed that he turned his back. And I clambered in.

It turned out that our vouchers had to be exchanged for tickets outside Grand Central Station. The only man in our

Reunions took place in large city train stations and whistle stops across the country. For the war brides it marked the dramatic conclusion to one journey and the exciting beginning to a new life.

group volunteered to locate the office and get all the tickets. The porters had placed our luggage in the centre of the floor, and our little party sat there, wearily waiting for something to happen.

I think I would have been sitting there yet if it hadn't been for those warm-hearted Americans. A lady asked me if I'd like some milk, then came back to suggest that perhaps a Coke (whatever that was) would give me more pep. Another lady was feeding milk through a straw to a crying baby; its mother had gone to enquire about a train to Winnipeg.

A man asked my destination and took off. He returned later with the Travellers Aid (who sent a telegram to my mother-in-law) and the news that I had ten minutes to catch the only train that night to Montreal. My baggage would have to wait until the next day, but if my ticket arrived quickly, the train would be held for me for five minutes. . . . We made it! My new friend, whom I never saw again, wouldn't leave until I was actually seated in an air-conditioned coach. After a whispered conversation with the conductor, someone gave up his seat for me.

The man sitting next to me was reading comics. What sort of a place had I come to where grown men read comics? He was normal enough and also kind. He moved to the smokers' carriage so that I could lie down on the double seat. I would have slept there quite comfortably if the conductor hadn't woken me every fifteen minutes to make sure that I was all right.

At 8:00 a.m. the following day I arrived at the old Bonaventure Station. My first impression of Canada had been via the back yards of Montreal's St. Henri.

On that particular day when I landed in Canada, the April weather wasn't kind. Halifax and the St. Lawrence looked grey and dismal. The country we travelled through struck me as the same. It was depressing, and I wanted to go home.

The ocean crossing on the *Aquitania* had been great, so it was disappointing when I took violently sick on the train the first night out from Halifax. The jolting of the airless train, the soot and the noise really got to me and I wondered what I'd let myself in for. Fortunately, I was well looked after by the people in charge, and in spite of the humid ninety-five degrees, I was fine by the time we reached Toronto.

Being a special bride train, our caravan drew a lot of attention along the way. Workmen would greet us with shouts of, "Has your man got a job?" and "Where do you think you're all going to live?"

Soon after our bride train left Halifax, four of us, destined for B.C., sat together in the dining car and ordered B.C. salmon for dinner. The waiter placed the salmon and vegetables in front of me, I neatly cut the salmon into four and we each took a portion plus vegetables. We'd just started to eat when the waiter arrived with three more huge pieces of salmon plus three more bowls of vegetables. We didn't know whether to laugh or cry; such large servings after strict rationing just overwhelmed us.

We west coast people found it interesting to observe the different ways the girls were greeted as they got off the train. The greetings could be divided into three main styles.

First, there was the big city greeting, which was frightfully formal. Husbands and in-laws were behind a barricade on one side, the brides carefully herded over to and lined up on the opposite side and a brass band and dais and VIPs in the middle. A musical selection from the band would be followed by speeches from the various big-wigs. Then, and only then, were the husbands allowed to walk over and claim their brides, who were given a quick peck on the cheek and rushed back to get lost in the crowd. What an ordeal.

Then there were the small community greetings, which were very informal and the most fun to watch. Everyone was relaxed and happy, especially in Quebec. One shy little blonde didn't want to get off the train when she saw the crowd of at least thirty people surrounding her husband. But he swept her off the train, gave her a passionate welcome and then she was passed from ample bosom to ample bosom. We decided that the coiner of the phrase "clasped into the bosom of his family" must surely have been French Canadian.

Finally there were the whistle stops, which made for rather sad reunions. In most cases just the husband greeted the bride, and they drove off in some sturdy vehicle into the icy wastes. On one prairie stop we literally couldn't see a building anywhere. They must have had a long, cold drive ahead of them. In the middle of the Rockies it was the same: we couldn't see any signs of civilization and we wondered how people lived so far away from the beaten track.

It was around February 5 when we said our goodbyes to girls going to Prince Edward Island and boarded the waiting train. The Canadian train was something else again. The luxurious comfort and gorgeous food were wonderful after those three gruelling weeks at sea.

Six of us had RCAF husbands awaiting us at Montreal. We were led up to the main concourse to be greeted by our worried men who had received no news of us during our long journey. It was a very emotional reunion.

Crowds were there to greet us. A band played, Red Cross officials were in attendance, newspaper reporters interviewed us and photographers took pictures. We were warmly welcomed by all sorts of people, officially and unofficially.

Then the six couples went to the hotel where our husbands had reserved rooms. It was a big hotel in the centre of Montreal. Old and elegant, it was favoured by the royal family when they visited the city. We were to meet in the dining room at six for a celebration dinner which the boys had arranged. Dressed in our best, we came down from our rooms to be treated like VIPs. It was all so wonderful, especially being with our loved ones again.

But another great thrill was to come. We all walked out of the hotel to have a look at Montreal, and there before us was fairyland. All the lights were on. Shop windows were lit up. Neon signs were flashing. And car headlights shone brightly. We hadn't seen lights at night for five and a half years, and it seemed incredibly beautiful. I shall never forget it.

After we left the ship we were taken to the Salvation Army hostel in downtown Halifax, and the first thing we did was to window shop. The stores were closed, but we enjoyed comparing styles and prices. My sister-in-law lived in Halifax and I received permission to stay overnight with her. Next morning the Salvation Army officer picked me up at 5:30 a.m. and put me on the 6:00 a.m. train for Sydney. The officer gave me my train ticket and two meal tickets. The meal tickets meant nothing to me. I was really timid in those days and didn't know about diner coaches and things. However, lonely and heartsick, I was nearing my destination.

After a few hours, I looked out and saw we were on the water. At MacIntyre's Lake I was transferred to another train where I was housed with the conductor in the caboose which was heated by a pot-belly stove. At Louisdale station, along with my baggage and steamer trunk, I was ushered into a tiny station building.

In Halifax we'd been told that there was no need to wire our in-laws to let them know we were coming because they would have been notified by the Red Cross. In my case, this hadn't been done. There was nobody there to meet me.

Louisdale was a small French-Canadian community, and children crowded around, curious about the stranger who couldn't understand French. Fortunately the station mistress spoke English and came to my rescue. While I was waiting, I noticed a cart drawn by oxen and three men who sported long fuzzy sideburns which were not in style at that time. Well, I thought, I've heard of the Woolly West—this must be it!

The mail carrier kindly offered to take me to Arichat, and there, outside the post office waiting for the mail, was my father-in-law. The mail driver told him that the good-looking dame with him just happened to be Valma's wife. He was so excited he jumped into the car and asked the mail carrier to drive us straight home. He bounded into the house shouting, "She's here, she's here." Then before his daughter could ask who *she* was, he'd run back out to fetch the luggage. That evening we heard that President Roosevelt had died. It was a date that I'd remember.

The house was situated on the lower road, overlooking beautiful Arichat Bay. I listened to the water lapping against the shore that night. It was such a lonely sound, and I was so homesick.

We were led at midnight through the vast immigration sheds and onto the train which would deliver us to our respective destinations across Canada.

The first food we were given in our new country was ice

cream and donuts. Apparently everything else had been given out to those ahead of us. I must confess that I thought it was a strange custom to eat such things at midnight, but when in Rome. . . .

It so happened that the coach to which I was assigned had only one other bride who was without children. This presented problems for the two of us. Needless to say, it was much easier for mothers to cope with children if their beds were left down instead of being made up. This meant that the other girl and I had nowhere to sit, since we were occupying upper berths. I have never felt so wretched in my life.

I had developed a cold and it was getting steadily worse. The cars were so dirty that we could hardly see out of the windows to look at our new land. In my misery it seemed as if the porter was continually appearing at the door and announcing a new time zone. "Put your watches back," he said. We'll never get anywhere, I remember thinking.

We kept stopping at different points to let off passengers. Often the Red Cross, bless them, came aboard with choice rosy apples and other treats. Before the first day was far advanced, the other childless bride and I had had more than enough. Neither of us wanted to see another child, let alone have any of our own. We couldn't sit in the washroom because it was festooned with diapers. We asked to see the major in charge of the train and informed him that unless we could have one berth made up so that we could sit down, we would get off the train and make our own way to our destinations. That brought the desired results.

Early in the morning of Thanksgiving Day we arrived at the old Bonaventure Station in Montreal. There was a band playing, the ropes were up and hundreds of relatives were there, waiting to see what they'd drawn in the great marriage lottery.

By this time I'd had it with the war brides and I decided that this was where I and they would part company. Whilst on the train I had received instructions to proceed to Ottawa and report to the chief neuro-psychiatrist of the DVA. There was to be a room awaiting me at the Lord Elgin

Hotel. I disembarked with my baggage, and by the time the authorities realized that I had done so, the coach with the Ottawa brides had left for Windsor Station.

A Red Cross driver took me over to the station and, at my request, found me a seat in the parlor car at the end of the train. We reached Union Station, Ottawa around noon. Again, there was a huge crowd of relatives on the concourse, the ropes were up and the military band was playing.

I grabbed a redcap and walked up as if I had nothing to do with the war brides and got into a cab. In those days cabs were scarce and one often shared with strangers. A couple climbed in beside me and the woman leaned over saying, "There's a terrible crowd at the depot this morning. I hear some more of those refugees have arrived." I turned to her and said, "Well, if you mean the British war brides, I am one of them." We lapsed into silence. A fitting finale indeed.

There was red tape and confusion when we arrived at Halifax, but we were eventually sorted out and hustled onto trains for our journeys into Canada. We found the trains hot and airless. And we noticed there were no leaves on the trees as there had been when we left England. I remember stopping at Rivière du Loup where most of us got out and tried to buy things. That was our introduction to French Canada.

I knew that my destination was Woodlawn, Ontario, a tiny place twenty-five miles east of Ottawa, but I didn't know that normally only freight trains stopped there. It was just a siding really, but our train was making a special stop for me. When we reached Ottawa, the attendant told me to get ready. It was 2:00 a.m., and I seemed to be the only passenger awake. I was nervous because I didn't know who or what to expect. I looked out the window as the train slowed down and there wasn't a light to be seen anywhere. The porter helped me down and swung his lantern. "Anyone there?" he called out. There was dead silence apart from the hissing steam of the train. Finally a Red Cross official got out and told me to get back on the train. I was taken on to North Bay, but I shivered and shook so much that I couldn't sleep all night.

In North Bay another Red Cross lady took me to her house and I went to bed. While I slept, my sister-in-law was contacted, and it was arranged for me to be met at Fitzroy Harbour, the correct station. The telegram about my impending arrival had not been delivered to my in-laws and they had no phone at that time.

That afternoon the marvellous Red Cross woman took me shopping and explained Canadian money to me. I bought two cotton dresses which were beautiful to my eyes. My clothes were crumpled from travelling and I didn't have many presentable things anyway because of clothes rationing. Later the lady and her husband took me to the movies. There was a newsreel about England and I cried. Just nerves, I'm sure. Those people were so good to me. They put me back on the train at midnight and this time I was met and all was well.

The journey by train from Halifax to Whitby was a nightmare for me; the baby had an ear infection and cried all the way. I remember one dear old porter who periodically walked her up and down the aisle so that I could rush and grab a meal in the dining car.

Many times during that ride I was to wonder why I had come all that way from home. It looked so desolate from the train window . . . all those old wooden buildings.

As the train stopped at each station we had to wait to make sure husbands or in-laws of war brides were there to meet them. One poor girl was not met and she was taken on to Toronto. We surmised that she would be sent back home.

Frankly, my first impressions of Canada were not too favourable.

I don't think I'll ever forget the train ride from Halifax to Toronto. The jerking and banging and the whistling at every crossing made it impossible to sleep. Not to mention the soot, the crying children and the frustration of not being able to open any windows.

In daylight I noticed the slummy-looking wooden shacks near the railway line in Quebec with poorly-dressed children begging for coins. And I wondered what kind of country I'd come to.

However, following the confusion at Union Station, Toronto, and in boarding the train for London, things began to look brighter. At London I was met by my husband and his employers who were my sponsors. I felt a lot more cheerful.

We drove out to the farm where we stayed for six weeks. In that time I had my first experience of a "shower". Jack and I had been fortunate to rent a furnished house and a friend would often drive us there to get it ready for moving in. One evening she persuaded us to take dressy clothes with us and said to get cleaned up before returning home.

On driving into the farmyard we saw lots of cars. I didn't think too much of it as the farmer umpired baseball games in the village and often had team members back to the farm afterwards. But when I went inside there seemed to be people everywhere, all shouting "Surprise!" They were such friendly, kind people and I still have most of the gifts we received that night.

The big moment arrived and we landed in Halifax. It was a miserable, cold, grey day, but I thought to myself, well this is Canada and here I am. I expected that Len would be there to meet me as I stepped onto Canadian soil. He wasn't there: he was waiting for me in Toronto. I had no idea the country was so enormous.

When we pulled into Toronto Union Station, I saw him before the train stopped. I couldn't believe it! He was in civvies and I'd never seen him in them before. He had on a double-breasted suit with padded shoulders, and I thought he looked like Al Capone. He hugged me and then he hugged the children, but I was still worried about whether we loved each other.

When we got to the apartment he'd rented he had a hundred dollars worth of lingerie waiting for me in this beautiful hope chest and an engagement ring. (We hadn't been able to buy one in England because of the luxury tax, so he'd promised me one as soon as I got to Canada.) I just looked at the things. I really didn't want to accept them until I knew how we felt about each other and whether we still loved each other.

Our apartment was on the east side of the Don River. On one side was the city dump and on the other the gasworks. It was a pretty run down area, but it was the only thing he could find.

Toronto looked very American to me. It almost looked like something out of a movie. There were so many neon signs in the downtown area that it seemed kind of gaudy and cheap.

Most days, Len would work until midnight or one o'clock in the morning. Before he went in the morning, he'd leave strict instructions that I wasn't to talk to any of the neighbours; he didn't want them to know our business. I spent the day by myself, looking after the children and then at five, I'd get the kids dressed up and make dinner and go down to meet him at the streetcar stop, hoping he wouldn't work late. I'd wait and wait for him to step off the streetcar, but he wouldn't be there. Finally I'd go back to the apartment and put the kids to bed. I've never felt lonelier. I think if I could have run back to mother then, I would have.

When we arrived in Canada our money was changed, and it was goodbye to pounds, shillings and pence and hello to strange coinage. We had a short time before boarding the train, and a group of us rushed to the nearest greengrocers. The owners were ready with bags of fresh fruit; they'd seen plenty of war brides and knew what we craved.

The train was my home for the next four days. At this point I must praise the Canadian government. I always say that I could have been blind, deaf and dumb and stupid and still would have arrived at my destination. We were so well taken care of—no worries about luggage, customs or any of the other irritations that beset the ordinary traveller.

On the train the brides with children occupied the lower berths. We had twenty-two children under the age of two in our coach, and they were all very well behaved. I was in an upper berth and spent the first night in a panic lest the thing closed itself up with me inside. You see, I suffer from claustrophobia. The ladies' washroom was reserved for ablutions and the men's washroom for all the diapers. The bunks were made up before 5:00 p.m. so that the little ones could go to bed. Then the rest of us would gather in the mens' washroom amid the diapers, where we'd smoke and pick the brains of our porter.

Because we were on a brides' special and had to give way to scheduled trains, our journey was slow. We spent considerable time on sidings, and sometimes wives destined for cities such as Quebec would be taken off and run into the city on a local train.

One morning there was great excitement; we were going to see Lake Superior. Being accustomed to Britain's small lakes and ponds, we didn't want to miss one of the Great Lakes we'd learned about in school. So we all crowded to the window to get a glimpse. Then, to our astonishment, we found we were still travelling along the shores of Lake Superior eight hours later. The first laugh at ourselves and another point driven home about Canada's size.

We travelled on through northern Ontario where the only signs of life were a few Indian cabins and small children waving at our train. We wondered where all the towns and cities were. We began a sort of game, watching each time the train stopped at a little hamlet to drop off a lone war bride, then discussing the husband and in-laws who met her.

We chugged along and eventually arrived at what was Port Arthur. The ladies of the town met the train with gifts and souvenirs, a very hospitable gesture. At Winnipeg we had two hours' wait and were allowed off the train with strict warnings to be back in time or we'd be on our own. It was May 24, 1946, and all Winnipeg seemed to be going on a picnic. We struggled across Portage and Main, feeling that the traffic was going the wrong way—it was a hair-raising experience. To our disappointment, all the stores were closed. One member of our party wanted to buy a dress to wear when she met her husband since her suitcase had been left behind at Southampton. We found one little dress shop where the owner furtively let us in, pulling down the blind. The girl in question had a fifteen-month-old boy with her and, as she was engrossed in finding an outfit, I took charge of Adrien. Being a worrier, I left first so as not to miss the train. With Adrien in my arms, I staggered back across the widest street I'd ever seen amid swirling traffic to the safety of the bride train. It occurred to me that should Adrien's mother miss the train, I would have to explain his presence to my husband.

Then I was on the last leg of the journey to Alberta. I can still see the beautiful prairie sunset and the lights twinkling in the distance across that flat prairie land. We were hot in the train, and someone decided to force open a window. What a mistake that was! We were immediately smothered in dust.

When we left Regina, I knew that my turn was about to come. I was to leave the train at Bassano, Alberta, some ninety miles east of Calgary. The last night was a sleepless one but, finally, with butterflies in my stomach, I was there. It was the only time that a train ever stopped just for me. Six o'clock in the morning, the sun already boiling, and there was this stranger in civilian clothes waiting for me.

And I knew that at every window on the train faces were peering out to see what I had married!

It wasn't very pleasant, that first impression of Fort Frances, Ontario. I'd come by train from Winnipeg and arrived at the uncivilized hour of 2:45 a.m. My husband's sister-in-law, bless her, just put her arms around me and said, "Welcome to Canada."

In spite of being thirty-five, I was homesick. Everyone was interested and pleased to see Bert's wife, for he had joined up a confirmed batchelor. He was born in Fort Frances and well known in the community. I met two or three English ladies and that helped, but it seemed an awful long time until Bert came home in September.

I journeyed to Cochrane in northern Ontario with my three-month-old son who'd been born after my soldier husband had returned to Canada. I'll never forget seeing my husband for the first time in civilian clothes. He wore a fur hat and looked like a Russian, especially against the Siberian-like background. Who is this stranger? That was my first reaction.

The snow banks looked ten feet high on either side of the road. In fact, we seemed to be going through a tunnel of snow.

My in-laws met me in a gorgeous Chrysler Imperial limousine. It was only then that I discovered my father-in-law was a rich man. He'd made a lot of money during the war in the lumber industry. He'd set up camps, probably employing a lot of men from other areas. That was how our district became so French Canadian. Settlers had come from Quebec to work and had stayed on.

Wealthy in-laws are not a guarantee of happiness. I had many problems. They had a beautiful home and we had to live with them because of a common problem then, the shortage of housing. I hardly ever went out that first winter. It was bitterly cold and having no transportation for the baby—and no help where that was concerned—I stayed in my room. Somehow I got the idea that maybe people didn't go out, that you'd freeze to death walking, especially with a baby!

People didn't call. *Nouveau riche* folks are not always popular. I was so lonely. I used to cry in my room, especially when hymn music came on the radio (I'm Welsh).

A young lass from Scotland also travelled to Cochrane. Her mother-in-law met her with the news that she had already been deserted. Her husband was living with another woman in Toronto. This mother-in-law was absolutely wonderful. She took the girl and her baby in, they stayed and the war bride went out to work.

In May I was invited to a small community called Island Falls to stay with relatives of a brother-in-law. Winter had gone and suddenly, without warning, it was summer. I was happy in Island Falls. The people were very friendly in that remote community which exists no more.

On arrival in Calgary, after much discussion, it was decided that I should detrain first. I declined and it was just as well —when I did get off that train I couldn't find my husband. I was near to tears when I saw all the others being greeted so warmly. And there was I, who'd been so sure of myself, all alone in a vast, strange country.

However, thanks to the Red Cross, it was straightened out in a matter of minutes. My husband was phoned: "Your wife is here, what are you going to do about it?" Reply: "Well, I guess I had better get down there." He had never received the cable to tell him of my imminent arrival. He knew I was in Canada but just where was the question. I have been told that the streets of Clive, Alberta, were the dustiest they'd been in a long time that day he rushed off to meet me.

Coming, as I did, at a time of the year when the Canadian landscape was at its most drab, while England was in the full beauty of spring colours, I am afraid that my first impressions of Canada were not very good. The countryside looked so dreary, not a green thing showing. The only splashes of colour to be seen from the train as it sped across Canada were from the multi-coloured roofs which I found quite attractive.

But, oh, that terrible train ride! To anyone used to the smooth-riding English trains, that ride was a nightmare and the roughest one I have ever experienced. We were almost thrown from our seats many times, and at one point in Ontario we thought there must have been a derailment. With startled cries of "What's happened?" and "Is it an accident?" heads peeped out from curtained bunks (for it was in the small hours) down the length of the train. After a long stop in the middle of nowhere, the porter assured us that all was well and that the engineer would likely be fired for his bad performance. Then he added, "He was driving freight trains before."

At stops across the land we were met by crowds of people. At first I thought how nice it was to get such a welcome. Then it dawned on me that there was little or no waving and cheering; they just stood and stared at us. I was to learn later that many, though not all, "just went to see what the war brides looked like". What had they expected to find? A train load of gaunt, emaciated, poverty-stricken women? Our wartime rations may have been meagre, but as a group we were neither starving nor poverty-stricken. As for our offspring, it was well known that the children of wartime Britain were exceptionally healthy; the government made sure they did not go short of vitamins, milk and other essentials for their well-being.

I came across many misconceptions among Canadians I met. One person went so far as to tell me that if I hadn't married a Canadian I would have had nothing. Yet I had earned an ample income and had had my own car, annual seaside holidays and money in the bank. My material wants were few. Some years later I was told bluntly why the war brides were resented by certain Canadians: "Of course we resented you. You hung around the camps until they had to marry you. You stole our men." I am inclined to a more charitable view now, but at the time, as a stranger 5000 miles from home, it was hard to take. Then again, I have always been too sensitive for my own good.

I remember a letter of welcome sent to all war brides by the wife of the Governor General. She said: "When asked how you like Canada and the Canadians, always say you like everything. Never criticize your new country or fellow countrymen, for you are now one of them." It was an excellent policy in theory but not easy to practise. We were criticized and felt we were justified in doing the same, or at least in defending ourselves.

My first over-all impression of the country was one of lavishness, both in its size and in the profusion of goods. We had been without things so long in the old country, while in Canada there seemed to be nothing one could not buy if money was available. And there were none of those endless lineups.

I really hadn't the slightest idea what to expect when I arrived in Quebec. We stayed three months in St. Jean and then moved to Drummondville where we settled. Of course, I'd known that my husband was a French-speaking Canadian, but it was quite a shock to find that his relatives spoke no English at all. Although his family was a bit put out that he'd married une Anglaise (and a Protestant one at that), they were very good to me.

I was very homesick the first year, and upset. My mother died six months after I came over, and my father died a year after that. I remember crying my eyes out when I saw my first baby, knowing that I could never show her to mum and dad.

Prior to settling in another part of the province, we spent two weeks with my husband's family in his home town, Valleyfield, Quebec. I was warmly welcomed by my in-laws, and the people of Valleyfield were extremely generous to me. I was honoured with showers of lovely gifts and feasts of food. The food part was somewhat frustrating because I couldn't eat a lot; we had been used to limited amounts of plain food.

But I was to develop one galloping addiction. We hadn't tasted bananas in years. I was always a fruit freak, and my sister-in-law introduced me to banana splits. I believe they cost thirty cents in 1946. For a year or two I was banana split mad, and my husband had to drag me past restaurants. I took to 7-Up, too, and in my first pregnancy he had to run out at all hours for more.

A kind word or a friendly wave did much for me in the early days, but I found it difficult to answer the frequent question, "How do you like Canada?" One just hadn't had time to find out.

I was terribly homesick at first and not very out-going. In our textile town at that time there seemed to be a degree of class distinction practised by some of the British-born people who held the better jobs. This wasn't apparent to me among the native Canadians. A lot seemed to depend on your husband's social status. My husband happened to be a new resident and starting work at the bottom. Fortunately, things changed as the old guard moved on.

We war brides had come to a new world in more senses than one. Our youthful years had been dominated by stern wartime conditions and it took me, for one, a while to adjust. It is difficult now to describe a certain impression I had at the time without seeming unjust to Canadians. But Canada and her people, in comparison to war-exhausted

Britain, appeared slightly frivolous to me. I remember thinking, most of them have very little idea what it was all about. It was an observation not a condemnation.

In any case, we were all thankful in the late forties to have the chance to get on with peacetime living in the generous young country, Canada.

I was immediately aware of how vast Canada was, and so much of it seemed underdeveloped and unpopulated. Cold too, in March, with snow all the way until we reached the Fraser Valley in B.C.

I found it very amusing to hear Canadians grumbling about the rationing they had to endure. For each rationed item there were plenty of alternative unrationed items. And no queues either.

Fabulous, friendly and helpful—that was the sort of reception given to me by Canadians. I have never felt left out or a foreigner, which I am. As the wife of my husband, I was extended every courtesy, as if I too had been born here on Cape Breton.

At first there were showers and surprise gifts for me. And as we worked hard building our home, whole meals were brought to us. This is a Polish-Canadian community, and every Polish man who'd known my husband pitched in and helped. They poured cement, measured and nailed down boards and painted shingles.

And when we moved in there was a house-warming to be remembered. We were given all sorts of things for home use. And the baking, wow! We had such a happy time going into our home. There were polkas and mazurkas. They danced so lively at my house-warming that a stove-pipe fell out of the wall.

I thought Canada had a strange smell. I have always been sensitive to odors and as I leaned over the ship's rail at

Halifax, I thought to myself, it doesn't smell like England at all. It seemed an alien place with an alien smell, and I wondered if I'd ever get used to it.

We arrived in Winnipeg after a dreadful train journey. At least it had been for me, suffering as I was from a bad case of motion sickness. We pulled into the station on a drearily dark and wet September morning. However the welcome I received from my husband's family and friends more than made up for the weather.

Coming from the seaside town of Worthing in Sussex, I thought that Winnipeg was a very dirty and ugly city. At first I had little feeling for the prairies in general, thinking the land very flat and lacking in beauty. Of course, fall was a bad time to view it all, and I was to have a vastly different impression when spring arrived.

I'm not likely to forget my first winter in Canada: the homesickness, the strangeness of everything and the problems with the baby, who was as upset as I was and refused to eat normally.

We had spent the first few months with my husband's family, but it was a small house and a large family, so we were anxious to get a place of our own. We finally moved into a big old house on the outskirts of the city. With accomodation being so scarce, we felt we were very lucky, even though the place didn't have sewer or water. All I had to cook on was a single burner hot plate. My knowledge of cooking was minimal and to learn the art on that single burner was doing it the hard way. Yet, having no preconceived ideas made it easier for me to learn to cook Canadian-style meals.

The only source of heat was a big black Quebec heater, and how I hated that thing. It was always going out on me at inconvenient times and, as my husband was away a lot, I had to cope with it on my own.

Yes, we suffered with the cold that year. I think I spent most of my time in overshoes and topcoat. To wash the kitchen floor was an impossibility at times because the water froze before the floor could dry.

Of course things improved as time went by, but I'll never

forget that winter if I live to be a hundred. The only saving grace was my dear mother-in-law who came to visit me without fail every Tuesday. No matter what the weather or how deep the snow, she'd make that difficult journey in order to spend the day with me. She had been a war bride of the previous generation and she understood what I was going through.

I left for Birsay, Saskatchewan to meet my husband's parents, while John stayed behind to look for accomodation for us in Winnipeg.

I changed trains at Saskatoon where Pete Brown, our best man, met me. It was funny to see him in civvies.

I was very nervous, and when my father-in-law met me at Birsay, he said, "All the village is here to meet you." I was the first war bride to arrive there and was treated like a movie queen. I'd never felt so important! The president of the local Red Cross made me a welcoming speech, and then I was off on a sleigh. I'd imagined sleighs would have small dainty horses with bells on, but this was a big stone boat drawn by an enormous work horse.

I was taken for a quick look round Birsay and then to the Brown's house. A tea had been arranged and the place seemed full of women. My father-in-law found Mr. Brown hiding under the kitchen sink!

My train had been late and they were all concerned about getting the tea over so that I could be driven the four and a half miles to the in-laws farm before darkness fell. I made the ladies laugh about some of the stupid things I'd done on the train, which included finding myself in the men's room. All too soon I was told that someone was ready with the sleigh. I replied that I was not ready. I have since learned that one does not keep men and horses waiting.

My mother-in-law had a lovely roast supper waiting. They were so kind to me. In fact, I think Saskatchewan people must be the kindest in the world.

My husband and his sister, who had been in England with the RCAF, had been honest with me about the good and the bad of my new country. But when I arrived in Bassano, Alberta at 6 a.m. I must admit I had second thoughts. The only person on the main street was an elderly Indian complete with braids. Later that day I met the fellow and he thought it a huge joke that he should have been the first one I saw.

After the reunion with my husband, the time came to meet "the mother-in-law". This involved a ten-mile drive across the prairie with nary a tree for mile after mile. I found myself thinking of the Sunday school hymn, "On those far hills, long cold and gray". While I felt very nervous, I realized that the occasion must be just as nerve-racking for her, meeting a daughter-in-law from afar. Jack, my husband's step-father, came in from farm work and I remember that, wanting to make a good impression, I grabbed his hand. He had not had time to wash, and his hand had cow manure clinging to it.

I had arrived on a Saturday and couldn't believe that the sleepy, sun-drenched main street was all there was to Bassano. Barrie showed me local sights which turned out to be the Bassano Dam (the motto of the town is "The Best in the West by a Dam Sight"). I kept wondering when something would happen. It being a Saturday, I didn't have long to wait. After supper at the only hotel—a lovely old building that I hope is never torn down—we ventured out on Main Street. I couldn't believe my eyes. The sleepy street had been transformed into a miniature bustling metropolis. I hadn't been prepared for Saturday night in a small town. The stores were open until 10:00 p.m. then, and all the country folk around had come to town to shop and visit. I'd had the mistaken idea that "backwoods" people would be dowdy. Not so. The street was literally jammed with vehicles of all shapes and sizes. Children spilled out of cars, shouting hello to their peers. Smartly dressed matrons were catching up on the week's news and buying bumper supplies of groceries. Ranchers were bantering back and forth about crops and cattle. How the metamorphosis took place was a mystery, but it was a community party out there on Main Street. I loved it!

My husband and I had two great days in Saskatoon when I arrived. We'd never had a real honeymoon in England, and those two days were all we could afford.

Then we took the train to his home town, Birsay, Saskatchewan. At that time it was an all-day trip to cover the hundred miles. What a welcome awaited us at Birsay station. I felt like the Queen of England! All the people of the village and surrounding farm area were there to welcome me. I met my in-laws, two lovely people who still had their Yorkshire accents.

After tea someone drove me "over town". We went into a small co-op shop, and I waited patiently. Finally I remarked, "I thought we were going over town." It was then explained to me that we were already in town. So I went and looked outside. All I could see was the one street with two garages, one cafe, one post office, one grocery store, one hardware store, plus the co-op. And that was it.

My first few weeks were spent getting acquainted with people and the different style of living. There was no hint of the loneliness and frustrations I was to encounter in the months ahead.

Canadians were very friendly and certainly made me feel welcome, but trying to understand one another was not always easy. In most of the places I went, war brides were few and far between, and I often felt as if I was a side-show attraction. They had a great time kidding me about the way I talked and about some of my sayings. And there were some who thought English girls were pampered and lazy. I had quite a time convincing them otherwise. They didn't understand that I'd never seen wood stoves, sad irons, coal oil lamps and numerous other things that I had to learn to cope with.

I was just beginning to get used to the heat and altitude in B.C. when my first husband decided to take me to visit his sister in Saskatchewan. He was hoping to make farming our future, and I was to get a first-hand look.

To me it seemed like the end of the world—great stretches of land and sky, neighbours and towns miles away.

I was scared of the livestock, the outdoor toilet didn't help matters and the quietness was something I wasn't used to. I'd come from Wolverhampton and for the first time I began to miss the things of home: the pubs, the movie shows, big stores, dances and the faster pace of life. The loneliness was unbearable at times and I became very homesick. I was also pregnant and physically ill. But I had to forget my misery and pitch in and help. Harvest was in full swing, and meals had to be prepared and taken out to the fields. Days were taken up with cooking and washing dishes, and there was no time for self-pity. I learned a lot from those days on the farm, but Saskatchewan was not for me. I don't think I'd ever have got used to the loneliness.

We went back to B.C. but were unsettled and decided to move in with the in-laws in central Alberta, the land of mixed farming. I wasn't prepared for the long, cold winter with bitter winds, drifting snowstorms and temperatures of 40 and 50 degrees below zero at times.

And living with the in-laws was not that easy. The house was cold and draughty. Water had to be hauled daily, along with wood for the stove and pot-belly heater. At night the heater had to be kept low as a precaution against overheating the pipes. In the morning we'd get up to frozen water pails and ice-cold floors. And there were the everyday problems of trying to cope until my husband found work. There were tears and depression from homesickness, especially at Christmas.

Our first son was born in the spring. His crib was a dresser drawer and at night his bottle was heated over a coal-oil lamp. Yes, there were times when I longed to be back in England, but the good times overshadowed the unpleasant ones, and I was determined to survive the elements and other trials so that no one back in England could say, "We told you so."

One wonders about the percentage of failures in wartime marriages. Many had followed such brief courtships. Among those who turned out to be ill-matched was a couple due to settle in Nova Scotia. When the war bride arrived at her husband's home she discovered that his father was black and his mother white. Her husband had appeared to be totally white. She turned around and left for England by the same ship on which she'd arrived. I met her at Southampton and listened to her story. I blame the husband for not being honest with her. She had been totally unprepared.

Rev. L. H. Sutcliffe was with the Canadian Army Corps of Military Staff Clerks during the war.

One or two unfortunate matches come to mind. Once, with great difficulty and a lot of string-pulling, I arranged transportation back to England for a well-educated librarian from Birmingham. While a resident in England, I had worked for one of the large shipping companies. I still had some contacts and that was how I managed it.

The girl's husband appeared in a totally different light when she saw him in Canada. And I'm sure she'd never seen the likes of his family before. When I asked him if we could discuss the situation, I found him vicious in his thinking and uncouth. He finally agreed to pay her passage back home "but not a penny more".

The day before this girl was to leave Oshawa she phoned me, very upset. She had contracted chicken pox. I knew that I couldn't get another passage for her; I also knew that there were people travelling with worse ailments than chicken pox. So we got her some calamine lotion, advised her to stay away from children and off she went.

She got her job back and is now happily married.

I helped another war bride, a lovely gentle girl who stopped in Oshawa on her way back to England. When she'd reached her Alberta destination (big ranch, cars, lots of money, so her husband had promised her) she'd been met by a hostile Indian mother-in-law.

Mrs. Gwen Wakeford of Oshawa, Ontario was one of many Canadians who met and helped the young war brides.

Most trains carrying servicemen's wives, coming from Halifax where they had landed from Europe, passed through Levis, Québec. We were notified beforehand when there were women and children getting off there, of their names and whether or not the husband was still overseas. I met a great many dependents.

Sometimes we had to wait hours for the train, often in the middle of the night. Once I remember a lady getting off with a child, expecting her husband to be there (he had been notified) but he was not there to meet her. The army tried to find him, and I don't know how it all ended.

Another time, I accompanied brides on a train from Montreal to Winnipeg. One lady told me tearfully that on arrival in Halifax she'd been presented with a telegram from her husband who was in Vancouver, saying that he did not want her any more. Of course, the poor girl was quite upset and didn't know what to do, but continued on to Vancouver anyhow.

Mrs. Gertrude Ingle was an officer of the VAD corps of the Canadian Red Cross during and after World War II.

I was born in Durham, England, so I had a bond with the war brides and really enjoyed my work with them. I should like to have been able to visit war brides in their homes a year or so later to see how well they settled. Judging by reunions on the stations, some looked to be truly mismatched.

One girl wanted to get back on the train. Her husband was sick, and she'd been met by a French-Canadian mother-in-law who spoke no English. The girl was headed for the "sticks" and hadn't realized it.

Another war bride expected her husband to meet her at Halifax, but a message was left for her to take the train to Truro. Nobody met her there, so she took a taxi to the address she had. The taxi-driver asked her whether she was sure that she had the right address. He watched as she was greeted warmly by an Indian mother-in-law.

The girl tried life on the reserve for a year. Her savings built a house, but at the end of the year she was ready to go home to London. The Red Cross took over her care and saw to her passage home.

Among the war brides were some of the toughest kinds of women, and they were occasionally met by gentle, well-bred men. I feel there must have been many heartbreaks.

Mrs. Winifred Turner worked as a Red Cross nurse, escorting war brides and children on the bride trains between Halifax and Montreal.

On the ocean we were separated from the young women, but on the train we mixed freely. I sat with a young lady and her baby boy. They were going to a small town in New Brunswick—I can't recall the name of it. She was very young and pretty, well-bred and neat as a pin. When she arrived at her destination I helped her off the train with her baggage.

Parked alongside the station platform was a wagon drawn by two horses. A young man sat on the seat. He just stared straight ahead and made no attempt to get down and help her. I assisted her onto the wagon and handed up her suitcases. The fellow didn't kiss or embrace her. He just looked straight ahead. As they drove off, she turned and waved goodbye. I thought to myself, in twenty-four hours she'll likely be pushing a plow or cleaning out cattle stalls.

When I got back aboard the train the boys were all laughing. To me it was no joke. I thought a lot about that girl and I prayed that it didn't turn out too badly for her— or that she soon went back home as a lot of others did.

Ex-Sergeant R. Goodson returned with the war brides to Canada in 1942.

Settling In

Old roots had been torn up, and now came the process, conscious or otherwise, of putting down new roots in an unfamiliar and often difficult land.

Most made a valiant attempt to adapt to their surroundings, however harsh, and to fit into their new communities—and most succeeded. A sturdy sense of humour often helped.

I wasn't excited about coming to Canada as were some who craved adventure. I guess I'd had enough adventure with the bombs: we'd lived next door to a Surrey aerodrome during the blitz.

My husband was fighting in Italy with the First Canadian Division when I was bombed out and made my application to come to Canada with my little one-year-old son. My visa arrived in 1944 and in November we boarded the *Ile de France*, en route to the New World.

We touched land at Halifax, then entrained for our destination, a small town in Gaspé, which I shall call Vallée Blanche. We arrived there with the first snow. Then came my first meeting with my husband's people who were true blue Québécois and spoke only French.

Vallée Blanche was tucked away amid snowy scrub, pines and firs. In winter it was pretty well isolated. Villages in the area were often only accessible by horse and sleigh. The railway linked us with Quebec City, but after blizzards, the trains were often several hours late.

Isolated and northerly as it was, Vallée Blanche was to my eyes a miracle of North American comfort: many houses had central heating; most had mod-cons which I had rarely seen, even in the richer houses in England—refrigerators, for example, and washing machines.

I was struck quite forcibly from the first by the way Quebec women loved their homes and delighted in adorning them with the creations of their busy fingers. They were always repainting them, too. The sparkling cleanliness and comfortable air in homes so impressed me that I wrote home about it until my mother wrote back in frantic frustration. "Do for goodness sake *stop* harping on the freshly painted and beautiful interiors of houses in Quebec," she pleaded. Her post-war home was poverty-stricken and shabby.

And they also had a great deal of pride in their children, whom I considered spoiled. Nothing was too good for them. My mother-in-law took me on visits to her friends in the fortyish age group. These ladies all seemed to have daughters around my age, and the daughters already had four or five offspring each and hoped for many more. They loved children and considered them a woman's greatest glory and a man's pride and joy. "Without them we have no future. Children are our most priceless national treasure," I was told.

The girls and women of Vallée Blanche had great poise and wore their smart clothes with flair. I must have struck them as odd-looking in my wartime clothes, which looked shabby and shoddy compared with the chic outfits they wore. My coat was not warm enough without a double lining and I had no winter overshoes. My practical mother-in-law soon fitted us out with warm winter clothing from her favourite Eaton's and Simpson's catalogues. It was like Christmas when all those wonderful clothes came: British clothes were rationed because civilian garments, along with many other products, had taken second place to war supplies.

Most of the families were inter-related. They'd lived in

the same area for three hundred years. I was the only stranger and the first they'd seen from England. Naturally my presence caused a stir. Everyone had a good look at this *étrangère*, peeping from behind their trim lace parlour curtains or through the crisp cretonne kitchen ones to do so.

I spoke French but not the same French as the villagers. They had picturesque ways of saying things, and it took me ages to understand what they meant. I'd met French people in France on brief summer trips across the Channel and on one longer stay in a chateau as a student teacher. But Vallée Blanche folks were unlike the French I'd met in France. They were more pioneering, tough and earthy, and, at the same time, simple, childlike, open, direct and blunt. They lacked the veneer of sophistication which so often conceals the real personalities of big city people. When they disliked something, they said so. On the other hand, they never hesitated to express their warm, almost wild enthusiasm. They'd hug and kiss relatives on Sunday visits and dance for joy, as if they'd not met for fifty years instead of just the week before. The family was sacred, and family visiting almost as sacred as the obligatory Mass.

The centre of the village was the big grey stone church. Everyone went on Sundays. Some went every day and during Lent, many went daily. They were drawn together at church like one large family.

I, too, was a Catholic from birth, but what I had known in England was a different and wider Catholicism. At my Surrey convent school we'd had Catholic girls from Uganda, Nigeria, Jamaica, Trinidad, Portugal, Italy and France, as well as a few Protestants and Jews.

But in Vallée Blanche there was a special brand of Catholicism. It was bound up in the mystique of *"la terre, les ancêtres, les pionniers, la langue, la race et la culture"*. Since I was a newcomer and couldn't share in these other enthusiasms, I didn't feel at home in the church. Although the ritual was the same as I had known, there were those other forces, especially *la culture Canadienne*, with its deep-rooted fear and hostility to strangers, directed particularly toward

les Anglais. "God must have made les Anglais, too" I told them, "For if he didn't, who did? The devil isn't a maker: he is a destroyer."

Mother-in-law was a fine woman with all the talents of a model Canadienne. But a shadow had fallen over her life. Her son, in the eyes of the villagers, had degraded himself by an alliance with *l'ennemi*. He had betrayed them by wedding une Anglaise. She was kind to me, but I was not on a level with une bonne Canadienne. Her joy in her fine family was dimmed by the fact that the eldest son had married out of the group.

It was not my fault that I had been born outside the charmed circle, not on the *sol sacre*. Yet I felt terribly guilty. I, a stranger and worse, une Anglaise, had dared to marry into the Chosen People. Well, I hadn't realized that it was such a crime until I landed there in Vallée Blanche!

We'd been in Vallée Blanche, my little son and I, for fifteen months when the war ended and my husband came back from Europe. He'd seen service in several war-torn countries, including North Africa. He was happy to be

Women who had been teachers or shop clerks found themselves hoeing vegetables and plowing fields on Manitoba mink ranches or Saskatchewan farms.

home again, and the village gave him a hero's welcome. It was as though he had returned from the dead. He found it difficult to pick up where his life had left off six years before; he'd been in a world of which the villagers knew nothing, a world of suffering and want and grief.

Soon after we were sent to Trois Rivières by the Department of Veterans Affairs for whom he worked.

Trois Rivières in the St. Maurice Valley was the first real town that I had seen in Canada (unless you count a glimpse of Halifax from the train). Vallée Blanche was a small rural community although it called itself a town; Trois Rivières was an industrial city, noisy and hot when we arrived there in August. I soon found it to be a larger edition of Vallée Blanche.

We lived in a little community outside the city. It was 100 per cent French. The humble folk were warm and hospitable and helped us to settle in, but in many ways it was the same as it had been further north.

I was walking along the street one day and met two pious ladies. Both averted their eyes from me instantly. Maybe my neckline was too low or my sleeves too short making me an object of scandal that hot day. More likely, they saw the Anglaise as the embodiment of evil. Such lessons had been handed down for three centuries.

It was lonesome for me. I never made real contact with

the small (and nowadays much smaller) English-speaking community. My social life was nil. Fortunately, the St. Pat's Convent nuns were very kind. They invited the twenty or so war brides (English, Belgian and Dutch) to a tea party each week. Some of the nuns were Irish, some were French. I look back on them as real Christians and truly good women.

I'd grown quite used to the loneliness after ten years and didn't care whether I was accepted or not. After all, we had had our personal troubles to struggle through. We were poor, but the worst of our trouble was the fight against illness and hard luck; in 1949 while living in Trois Rivières, we lost a dear little son of leukemia.

It was hectic, raising a family of three while working at any odd job that came my way. That, plus fighting the long weary war against prejudice, was almost too much. And I had to try to accept the fact that poverty is equated with weakness in North America and that to be without one's own family in French Canada means aloneness.

But the barriers finally came down.

In 1945 the ordinary Québécois had seen little of the world outside of Quebec, but about 1960 they began taking to world travel. They proved wonderfully appreciative travellers and thrilled to the new places. And TV had come to open another window on the world. Quebec was no longer the isolated fortress barricaded stoutly against dangerous, outside influences.

Since I first came to French Canada in the 1940s, I have made my share of faux-pas. Especially at first. It must have been hard for my neighbours in Vallée Blanche to accept a stranger who had so little sympathy with their ways. But in time my mind was stretched and I grew less narrowly prejudiced.

I am happy that newcomers are being welcomed into the French-Canadian community now, instead of being feared and shunned. And that religion is more truly Christian here in Quebec today.

Canada has dealt me some hard blows, but I owe her a

lot. She has knocked off some of my rough edges and added a certain polish. Canada has shaped and civilized me, but maybe she hasn't finished the job yet!

I had no English when I moved in with my husband's family in 1946. We first lived outside a Nova Scotian town.

We soon moved to a room in the home of friends and then to a farmhouse. In that place we had no water and no electricity; I was expecting our first child. Later we were out of there and into a two-room house, and my husband found some work at a sawmill in the woods. He left me the first time when our second baby was on the way. I was very unhappy and the United Church minister offered to collect money to send me back to my family in Holland. I shall never forget the kindness of the ladies of the United Church who brought us food, or the lawyer who gave me ten dollars to buy milk.

My husband came back declaring that he was sorry. We next went to live in an isolated shack where there were no neighbours for ten miles. By 1950 we'd had four children in four years and we were living near his mother in another two-room place. We had no toilet there. We used the woods. I had to walk half a mile to get a bucket of water.

It was a great improvement when we moved into town and had electricity and well water. My husband decided to rejoin the army. I stayed where I was. Then the house we rented was sold and I had to move. With more help from sympathetic United Church people I moved into two rooms which were converted from a garage. There we had to share a neighbour's bathroom. In the meantime my husband turned up—absent without leave. For the sake of our children I telephoned the military police in Halifax, and they picked him up. Our next move was to army quarters in Kingston, Ontario.

Our fifth child was born and six weeks later we were all on our way to Germany where my husband had been posted. The army paid our way, and the three years spent over there were much better for me and the children.

When he left the army we returned to Nova Scotia where he worked trailers and we kept moving.

Things got really bad in our marriage. He left me five times in all. I had to call the police because of physical abuse; after one beating I was confined to hospital.

I worked for two years in a laundromat, and the owner saved my wages so that I could go to Holland for a visit in 1969. I had never told my mother of my hardships in Canada. It was strange to be back in Holland again and at first I had trouble speaking Dutch. After a few days though, it was as if I'd never been away.

The marriage ended in divorce, but in spite of past troubles, I love Canada. I don't think I could live in Holland now.

It was many years before I could find any beauty in this country, but not long before I realized the kindness of Canadian people.

In 1944 Jean, my newly-commissioned husband, was returned to his regiment to take part in the final big pushback of the Germans in Europe. With my two little girls, I found a flat in LaSalle, Quebec, overlooking the St. Lawrence River.

Steep stairs led up to the front door, with a little cellar halfway up. The door at the top automatically locked when closed. There were connecting stairs to the apartment above and to my landlady's home via a glass porch on the river side of the building. So when a fire started beneath my porch I was able to run up the two flights to warn others and to phone for help.

Unfortunately, the fire followed me and I was prevented from returning to my babies by the same route. By the grace of God, the grocery boy had left my front door ajar, allowing me to get back into the apartment. My neighbour and I carried the little girls out to safety before everything was destroyed. I made one feeble attempt to return for my new fur coat but was unsuccessful. The fire left us with nothing to wear but our house clothes. It was December and we had no insurance.

Soon boxes of clothing began pouring in and the eighty dollars in cash that I received from well-wishers bought winter suits for the children. But I looked like a scarecrow for a year.

Accomodation was hard to find in Montreal at the time. A friend took me into her home in Brockville until I was fortunate enough to get an apartment in Toronto. I felt quite at home there until the war ended and we returned to Montreal. My kind landlady had re-built part of her burned-out property and saved a little section for us.

It wasn't long before overcrowding (with number three daughter having arrived) pushed us into buying land in the then village of Côte St. Luc, where we happily built a house around ourselves. There we had picnics in the fields and picked wild fruit for jam. Once more Canadian kindness smoothed the way; no waiting to be introduced there!

Our two boys were born and our village became a city. Despite my ties with Canada, homesickness for green England set in once more, and frequent trips back to the U.K. did nothing to alleviate it.

When our family was grown Jean and I returned to the land once more. We found a little orchard high on a hill in Franklin, Quebec. It boasted a small summer house and, after three years of weekend visiting, we sold our home and moved out to start "pioneering" again. Out here people still concern themselves with each other. I don't know how we would have managed if new friends had not given us storage space for our furniture while we insulated and extended the house.

Nearly two-thirds of my life has been spent in Canada and our children are bilingual Canadians. I've travelled the Maritimes extensively, taken a short trip out west, lived in Ontario, vacationed in the Laurentians . . . but my heart remains in Sussex, England.

It was May 1945. My husband was still overseas, and I'd arrived in Woodlawn, near Ottawa, to stay with my sister-in-law and her husband. They were middle-aged farm people and lived in an old log house with his elderly father. They had 200 acres of land, cattle, horses, barns and the rest, but there was no electricity and plumbing. I had to get used to all that. I got on well with them and they were kind, thoughtful people. For instance, the first Sunday I was there, they took me to the Anglican Church because they knew the service would be familiar to me.

I made up my mind that I'd learn all I could about the Canadian way of life in case we ever had a farm of our own. I watched how my sister-in-law shopped and cooked and I helped with the baking. I also spent a lot of time with old Dad, a retired carpenter. He loved to play jokes. One hot evening he told me that if I stayed very quiet, I'd see his favourite wild animal come to visit. He was standing by an old shed, leaning on a shovel. After a while a small black furry animal came out from under the shed. The old man whacked it with a shovel and killed it. Of course, you know what the skunk did. I'd never heard of such an animal but the old man thought it a great joke and laughed

Sharing experiences with other war brides made the adjustment to Canada easier—and led to some life-long friendships. Right, the "Always Be Friends Club" at a picnic in Springbank Park, Ontario in 1948; below, the War Brides Group in Winnipeg, Manitoba in 1950; left, the British War Brides chapter of the IODE in Victoria, B.C. in 1947.

uproariously. He didn't care about the stench because he'd lost his sense of smell, but I was sick right there.

My sister-in-law kept bees. She had about thirty hives, and a clump of rhubarb grew close by. We'd been informed that my husband would be coming home from overseas and we could meet him at a parade in Lansdowne Park a few days hence. Violet decided to welcome her brother home by baking his favourite pie, rhubarb and lemon, and asked me to go and get some rhubarb from the garden. I did and the bees attacked me. I was badly stung, especially around the eyes, and the day I met Cecil from overseas I looked as if I had two black eyes. I felt kind of foolish but proud and pleased, too.

We moved to Cecil's old home where his father and brother lived. It was threshing time and I was to provide threshing meals for the men. This was the first time I'd really had to do things on my own. Although I had difficulty coping with the woodstove and sometimes ran out of supplies, I did the best I could and managed to produce satisfactory food of the traditional kind for fifteen men.

Then I became pregnant and a bit homesick. I had not expected so much snow and wind in winter and I hated it. The old house was cold, and after Christmas we went back to Woodlawn to be nearer a hospital. When my baby was stillborn, I thought it was a calamity. But in retrospect it was for the best: I was not ready to look after a baby.

That summer we found a hundred-acre farm for ourselves. It was four miles west of Luskville on the Ottawa River. The house was nice and just what we wanted, but it took every penny we had, as well as DVA grants and loans. We had a team of horses, a few cows and a few pigs for a start and we scrounged furniture from all the relatives and were given a shower by the neighbours and church people. Those were lean years. We shipped milk to the local cheese factory, but within five years it closed down, and we had to sell cream for butter making. Then disaster struck.

On January 6, 1949, when our daughter was six months old, Cecil got up early to milk the cows as usual and lit the kitchen stove before going out. Half an hour later I arose and put on my dressing gown. I opened the kitchen door and to my horror, the wall behind the stove was alight. I tried to put it out with the fire extinguisher to no avail. I grabbed a coat, wrapped the baby in blankets and rushed out in my rubber boots. I yelled to my husband who came running. Then I waded through snow well over my knees to a neighbour who had a phone. I left the baby with her and, with legs nearly frozen, went back to get a few things out through a window. The house was burning furiously and we couldn't save much. Deep snow hindered the fire equipment, and there was only well water to use anyway. I lost everything that I'd brought from England and the wedding presents we'd received in Canada.

The neighbours were great. They held a benefit night and all sorts of things were given to us. Some of the local men got together and built us a tiny two-room house. We stayed with a neighbour until it was ready.

We lived in that little house until our son was nearly four and it was no longer big enough for us. During that time I tried to pay back those good folks who'd helped us. I was unable to do it with money, but I think I managed through giving my services to local organizations. I took offices for long spells as both president and secretary of the Women's Institute and the church group and I also taught Sunday school.

I came to Canada in the summer of 1945. I was twenty-four years old, very English and very green. I remember being thrilled and amazed at the smartness of everything. There was nothing shabby or war-weary about the people, their clothes, the food or the buildings.

I spent the first six months in Montreal with Bert's parents in their Notre Dame de Grace duplex. It was a difficult time. Bert started work at his old job with a textile company at forty dollars a week. I spent my time getting to know his family and Montreal. Bert was one of five brothers, all very different in temperament, all very headstrong.

His father was of the old school and expected obedience in the Victorian manner, while his mother seemed to spend her time acting as peacemaker. It was not a happy household, and I was glad when Bert was promoted and transferred to Drummondville. It was to be the first of many moves we would make over the years.

We took a train and spent our first few weeks at a hotel. Eventually we found a room with a French family.

How hard it was to find an apartment. The one we found was on the main street over a store. It is gone now, burned down. That was our first real home. Then some little houses were built on the north shore of the St. Francis River. We bought one and had to borrow three hundred dollars to make the down payment. What a time we had trying to pay that back. It was as difficult as paying back three thousand would be today.

After that came Sherbrooke, Quebec. I hated the place. Fortunately Bert was thinking of leaving the textile business. He found a job and off we went, Bert and I and our young daughter, to the wilds of Quebec. We lived near the town of Mont Joli, in an old air force barracks, and it was a strange life; lots of parties, plane rides and lots of space for the kids. It was a startling change from the nine-to-five existence in towns and cities.

When construction wound up we moved across the river to the bustling boom town of Sept Iles. We were allotted a tiny house on the base camp (Mile One on the new railroad) about five miles from that town. After a year, a larger house became empty and we moved into that. I took a job handling the telephone exchange for an iron ore company starting work at 11:00 p.m. and finishing at 6:00 a.m. Despite the hours, the money was good. When the railroad was completed we moved into town—house and all.

Then I started to write a regular column for a local newspaper and also worked part time in a dress shop. Bert went into business for himself, hoping to cash in on the boom-town atmosphere of the place. He did quite well, but not well enough.

Our next move was to Ottawa, where Bert worked for a small airline. We were back in civilization. We started off in an upper duplex and after about two years found a tiny house on an old farm property in Alta Vista. It was like a little coach house. Our daughter was by then in junior high school, and I found work through Office Overload. I even learned something about aerial survey mapping and was hired by the airline to contour maps. It looked as if we might settle down.

And then Bert was offered a job with a helicopter firm in Montreal. This time we managed to buy a house, a new house. We moved in and we were there exactly nine months when Bert was transferred to Winnipeg. I was left to wind up things in Montreal. I rented the house, got rid of a lot of junk, shipped the furniture, packed the car and drove out to Winnipeg.

Our first home in Winnipeg was a rented bungalow. A year later when the owner returned from the States, I had to find another place. Another bungalow, another move.

When our daughter finished high school and went into university, I decided that it was time for me to get a full-time job. I had done some freelance writing for newspapers and the CBC and managed to land a job with a commercial radio station.

My marriage broke up. After a month in a motel, my daughter and I found an apartment. I continued to work and was lucky enough to get an offer of a higher salaried job at a TV station. Later on, another offer came from an advertising agency, a big raise this time. Each move meant financial improvement and promotion. Eaton's approached me several times, and I eventually accepted. I am still with them.

Nineteen forty-five to 1977—it seems like a lifetime. Do I love Canada? You bet I do. I think it's the finest country in the world. Any unhappiness incurred over the years was of my own making through lack of experience and a great deal of indecision. Canada has been good to me.

Funny situations arose as I struggled to change some of my English words for Canadian. Trousers had to become pants, lifts gave way to elevators, pavements to sidewalks and so on. But the expression that got me into the most trouble was the innocent English phrase, "to knock up". Here in Nova Scotia it is considered a vulgar term for getting a woman pregnant.

We spent our honeymoon with a dear friend, a woman who'd known me since childhood. She had cooked us a special breakfast that first morning. Henry got up first and went downstairs while I slept on. "Where is Hilda?" asked our hostess. "Still sleeping," answered my new husband. "Well, then," she told him matter-of-factly, "you go and knock her up." My startled Canadian husband replied, "Holy Cow! So soon!" We often laugh over that one.

Later, my husband was to go on a trip to Halifax as a passenger in a neighbour's car. He arrived back at 3:00 a.m. The door was locked and I was fast asleep. He awoke me by rapping on a window and I let him in.

Next day the wife of the car driver called in. She asked, "What did you think of Henry coming home at that time?" I retorted, "What would you think if your husband came knocking you up at three in the morning?"

Poor woman, I'd given her a cup of tea and she very nearly dropped it in her lap!

In time I did learn to avoid using that expression.

We looked around for land to buy in order to start a mink farm and were lucky enough to find forty acres of bush near Peterfield in Manitoba, about forty miles north of Winnipeg. The land had a creek on two sides and the point was on a lovely bay. A mile down the creek were the Netley Marshes, which were famous for duck hunting.

The house on the property was just a summer place, but we had it insulated before winter set in. It was a very different home from the one I'd left in England. I had lived on a street of twenty-six houses, and now my nearest neighbour was a quarter of a mile away. Other people who lived along the creek visited back and forth by canoe. One of them happened to be an English war bride from London.

Starting a mink ranch took quite a lot of capital, and it was a few years before any real profit showed. When I talk of things I didn't have at that time, it is not in a complaining sense but just to show how different the way of life was. One thing is certain—the early days of that hard life brought out strength of character that I hadn't known I possessed.

During the first year we had no electricity, only a wind-charger and storage batteries. If there was no wind, a Coleman lantern was our source of light. Many a time I prayed that the wind would blow, especially when I had sewing to do. Nor did we have running water in the house. Drinking water came from a pump and it was as hard as iron. We had a large tank to catch rain water which was used for dishes and washing. How thankful I was when detergents came on the scene.

When snow arrived at the end of October there was another new experience in store: I had to melt snow for water. So I filled a big copper boiler with snow only to find that it produced only about an inch of water. I learned that you had to get the hard-packed blocks from drifts, not the soft stuff.

Once I knew how to dress for it, I found the Manitoba winter exhilarating. But all that whiteness for so long—that got to me sometimes. Then I'd put on my winter togs and make my way up and down the snowdrifts until I reached the main road. Another two miles and I was in the village visiting my friends. Thirty degrees below zero weather didn't stop me: only a blizzard could do that. After these trips to town I'd be content again for another three weeks or so.

We didn't have much money but we sure were warm. Most winter nights I spent knitting pure wool socks, mitts and tuques. And I made ski pants from old melton cloth coats. Indians came to help with the mink at pelting time, and they told me to get the children into moccasins with three pairs of woollen socks.

Our fuel was wood from our forty acres of poplars. If our supply was low and Stan was too busy to haul wood, the children and I dragged out dead trees and I sawed them up.

Over the years we kept chicken and rabbits and one pig. It was a little runt that a farmer didn't want. We fed it up, and after it was killed I read leaflets from the Agriculture Department on how to make bacon and hams. The results turned out well. My folks in England could hardly believe the things I was doing.

Sure, there were times when I lost heart. Things would go wrong with the mink and we wouldn't get the price we expected. "Well, next year will be better," we'd tell each other. Sometimes I wondered if Canada would always be a next year country.

My husband's family was there to meet us, and we completed the last few miles of the long journey to Saskatchewan in their farm wagon. We were bumped and jolted over the deep frozen ruts of a dirt road before we reached the farm which was to be my new home. Only then did I begin to wonder what kind of life lay ahead of me.

It was unfortunate that I had not been allowed to mix with other people during my early years. As a result I was always terribly nervous about meeting strangers and found it very difficult to adjust to the rough and ready world in which I suddenly found myself. Saskatchewan was harsh climate and hard work country. The people had little time for refinement or polish or an understanding of the sensitivity of others. "That is sissy stuff," I was often told. I hasten to add that this was not the attitude of all. I thank God for the good friends I made.

The family and neighbours made me welcome, and I thought them very kind when they held a shower for me.

From well-tended English towns and bustling
European cities, many war brides found themselves
thrust into life in small towns or farms where the
conditions were primitive and the loneliness
sometimes overwhelming.

I received gifts of all kinds. Even so, due to my shyness, I
found it an ordeal to meet so many people at once. Try as
I would to adapt to the new ways and standards, I always
felt a misfit.

The best I could do was to take my new responsibilities
as a farmer's wife seriously. I was not afraid of hard work
and it was not long before I received my initiation into the
role with the job of mixing and hauling cement as we en-
larged our house.

I was a keen gardener; in fact I had taken a four year
course in it during my teacher training. It was my job to
work almost an acre of vegetable garden. I could not live
without flowers—to me they were part of the food for the
soul—and over the years I created a real English garden
around the house with lilacs, and with perennial borders
of irises, lilies, aquilegia, peonies, Michaelmas daisies and
chrysanthemums. At last I felt I had a little bit of home
with me, but the combined operations of tending vegetables, flowers and large expanse of lawn, meant eight hours
a day in the garden. We worked from 4:00 a.m. until
11:00 p.m. during the growing season. It was a far cry

from teaching! And in spite of all that, I kept my home clean, did lots of canning and made some of my own and some of my boys' clothes.

I missed my church and music and, believe it or not, I missed the gentle English rain. I was, in short, very homesick for the beauty of my homeland.

My husband was a very community-spirited man who served on several committees and was away from home frequently. At those times I felt very lonely. In the new world, community life seemed to play a bigger role than family life, a fresh concept to me.

Although I liked gardening, sometimes I would get discouraged. Either the cows would get into the garden and trample it down or else the pigs would eat it. One Monday evening, after a hard day with the washing and other chores, I noticed that our 120 pigs had found their way out of the corral and were heading for my garden. I knew they would go back to the barn when it became dark, but if they found my garden first there would be nothing left by nightfall. My husband was away at a meeting so I tried four times to get them back into the corral, each time finding a new hole in the fence and fixing it. By then I was exhausted and weary enough to drop. In desperation I phoned my husband with a plea for him to come home

and get the pigs into the barn before dark and check the fences. If he didn't, I threatened that I would start shooting the animals. By the time he arrived home I was too tired to get to the house and was sitting on a rock in the corral, crying. I liked the country life but how I hated the livestock!

By God's grace and our hard work we did well on the farm. When combines took the place of threshing machines I became my husband's hired man until the boys were old enough to help. I look back with pride on that first year when I hauled from the combine. It was an extra heavy crop, and my husband said he didn't want to stop the machine all day, not even for unloading. This meant driving the truck only a few inches from the tractor unloading as we went along. At that time we had no hydraulic hoist in the truck so each load had to be shovelled off. In between I ran around gathering straw with which to line the open bins which we used when all the granaries were filled. We never stopped work to eat: we devoured sandwiches on the run. I know lots of women who have done similar hard work but they were born here and used to it. I was thirty years old before I was initiated.

I will never forget my introduction to driving the self-propelled combine. My husband had been asked to act as pall bearer twice in one day. Not wishing to lose the benefit of the good weather, he returned home to work after the morning funeral. Then, before leaving again in the afternoon, he gave me a very short lesson on how to run the combine. As I remember it, the instructions went something like this: "If you pick up a root or a stone, immediately push the electric stop with one foot, step on the clutch with the other, pull the combine drive with the right hand and throttle with the left." With that, I was left to it. I can assure you I proceeded very cautiously.

In 1955 my husband sent me home for seven months. I was heading for a nervous breakdown, and he thought a trip home might help me. It was wonderful to see the greenness of home again and to hear the church bells once more. I was picked up where I left off and felt as if I'd never left England. The nine years in Canada seemed just a dream. The boys attended school in England; they were very happy there and wanted to stay.

During the winter following our return to Canada, we had the biggest blizzard I can remember. The school bus became stuck in our lane, and the men carried the children down to our house. That night I had twenty-four unexpected guests to feed and sleep. It was a wild night with a howling wind, and I was afraid of a chimney fire. (At that time we had only wood and coal heaters.) I was rather low on food supplies so at 4:00 a.m. I made a big batch of bread. No sleep that night! From that time onward I would stock up with extra food if there were signs of a storm, just in case the bus got stuck in our yard again.

Farm life was not all work. During the long winters we were free to pursue our personal interests. Although unable to join a choral or drama group, I could indulge my interest in handicrafts, especially dressmaking and woodwork. And I had time to catch up on my reading, including books I'd brought from home.

As the years went by, progress brought power and a pressure system to the farm. Work on the farm became

somewhat easier, especially with the help of our boys, and we were able to plan vacations. I particularly enjoyed the mountains, the Jasper area the most of all. But it was on Vancouver Island that I felt at home. There, the climate suited me better and the profusion of English flowers was a joy to behold.

When I arrived in Canada, my husband and I spent the weekend in Bassano, Alberta, getting to know each other again. Then we went on to Calgary for my twenty-first birthday. It was a fascinating trip for me; there was ninety miles of gravel roads and the entrance to Calgary was a small wooden bridge which allowed one car at the time.

Calgary was truly cowtown, and only 80,000 souls. My first impressions of the city were of old street cars, frilly-curtained houses resembling doll houses, men with open-necked shirts, riding boots, cowboy boots and wrapped bread, peanut butter and a strange food known as corn.

A trip to the Rockies and Banff was soon arranged, but the prairies, vast and lonely, affected me more than the mountains. The mountains were breathtakingly beautiful, but the lonely prairie tugged at my emotions, making me feel happy and sad at the same time.

My husband had a travelling job at the time and I went with him. I saw a great deal of rural Alberta and I recall that the talk was all about rural electrification. I found it hard to believe that people were still using oil lamps and outhouses. Eventually we settled for a time in, and then near Erskine, Alberta. We ran a service station, and my job was to man the pumps while my husband attended to the mail run. One day, while trying to give service with a smile, I almost filled a radiator with gas. The car was an old Model A, and I didn't know that the gas tank cap was on the hood below the windshield. Life was exciting then; there were always new challenges to be met.

When we went into farming, my ignorance made me the butt of many a joke. One time my in-laws had me believing they had to milk 200 head of range cattle that had just been weaned. I envisioned a wild cow-milking contest to end all. My new experiences included chasing cows and jackasses, learning how to separate milk, how to cook on a coal and wood stove and how to chop wood. I was fast becoming an efficient farm wife, when Barrie developed malaria (a legacy from service in Italy) and hay fever at the same time. So we left the farm and he turned to road work.

During these wandering years we lived in a variety of places. At one time our home was an airplane packing case, measuring eight feet by forty, and we managed to make it into a liveable building. Two of our children were born while we lived there. Our "home" was out in the bush, and we were surrounded by wild roses and saskatoon bushes. The beauty of it all made up for the rather strange living quarters.

Naturally, we didn't have running water, and I had to use ingenuity to conserve consumption. One method was to bury all soiled diapers in a hole, then just before wash day dig them up, scrape them with a special knife and wash them.

In retrospect those were happy times. It was seven years

and three babies later when we finally lived in a more civilized manner, but I wouldn't have missed the earlier life.

Things ceased to amaze me as I became Canadianized.
My father had given me a piece of advice on my departure in 1946 which stood me in good stead. He told me
never to forget where I came from but not to seek out
only war brides for friends. He said that I must mix and
become truly Canadian in order to be content. I have been
grateful for that advice.

I was also determined that our marriage should not fail
because I had too much pride and English bull-headedness
to admit that maybe I'd made a mistake. I suppose in
every marriage there comes a time of questioning, but I'm
glad I stuck out the lean times, the worst times. The good
times certainly outweigh them.

Apart from the usual adjustments to be made when settling
in a new country, I had to cope with the fact that my
husband was a Japanese Canadian and that his parents
spoke very little English. We had to live with them until
our own home was ready, and communication was difficult
at times.

Many of the social events that we attended in the early
days were parties at which no knives or forks were used.
The guests were all Japanese Canadians, and I had no
choice but to learn how to use chopsticks. It was either that
or go hungry.

At that time the whole family lived at home, all eight
brothers and four sisters. We ate together at a huge oval
table and meals were seldom peaceful. This was one family
that enjoyed a good discussion, and the only time they were
all together was at the table. I used to sit cowering in my
chair while all those people argued loudly about the merits
or faults of various cars, baseball teams, tractors, milking
machines and so on—things about which I knew nothing.

I had become an Alberta farmer's wife and that was my

second major adjustment. Until then I had been a city slicker and an office worker, doing nothing more strenuous than pushing a pen.

To start with we had one cow, chickens and a few pigs. Therein lay lesson number two—how to take care of those critters. My first and last attempt at milking was a disaster. The silly cow stepped on my foot for starters—she probably didn't like the names I called her—and she wouldn't drop her milk. Feeding the pigs and chickens was easier. Easier, too, than doing my housework.

At first the house had no water, not even a pump. All my life I'd merely had to turn a tap and water came out. Now the water was outside in a huge concrete cistern, and I had to haul it up in a bucket. In those days I weighed ninety-eight pounds with my clothes and shoes on, and anyone watching me heaving those pails up, teetering on the edge of the cistern, might have been tempted to place a bet on whether the water would come up or I would go down. After a few weeks of this, we installed a pump and life was easier.

And then there was the monster of a coal stove to tame. I was given some vague instructions by my husband. "You put in some newspaper and kindling, light that and then add the coal," he said. "Keep the damper open until the coal starts to burn." I didn't know what a damper looked like, but not wishing to show my ignorance I opened up everything that looked openable, including the ash box. Now anyone can tell you that if you open the ash box you will get a draught of air that will cause your fire to put Vesuvius to shame. Before I could say "Call the fire department", I had a red hot stove and only one idea on how to cool it down. Water! That was the stuff to put fires out, wasn't it? I quickly learned that you don't throw water onto the conflagration in a fire box or you get a mighty WHOOSH and the whole place, including yourself, gets covered in particles of soot and ashes. Oh well, live and learn. Yet I still hear talk of it in these parts. "Remember the time you tried to put the stove out with water?"

My education was advancing rapidly. Having weeded row after row of beans and potatoes a few times over, I was finally ready to gather in the crops. Ever picked beans by the acre? If not, I can tell you there is no easy way to do it. If you kneel and shuffle along, even with pads on your knees, they will feel like raw meat at the end of the day. If you stoop and walk along the rows, then your back will seem to be broken. You may try taking a cushion along to shuffle forward on your rear end. That may sound more comfortable but take it from me, it isn't.

After the beans, it was time to harvest the potatoes. Until we could afford the necessary machinery, the picking was all done by hand. The potatoes were dug up by a contraption behind the tractor and then the pickers gathered them up in sacks. This meant a lot of stooping, and at the end of the day, I felt that I'd never be able to straighten up again.

I thinned, hoed and weeded the sugar beets, but the harvesting was something else again. They are harvested after frost in the fall. Since the days are chilly then, the work is uncomfortable as well as hard. One year wet weather delayed digging, and it was Christmas before we had the beets stacked in piles for accessibility and protection from freezing. I was pregnant and recall struggling into my parka, barely able to zip it up. We were three in family by then and we headed out to the field armed with beet knives, which are something like machetes, with wide blades and hooks on the ends for grabbing the beet.

Field mice had ensconced themselves in the stacks of beets, obviously recognizing handy food and shelter. As soon as we attacked a pile they'd scatter in all directions, and at each new pile the mice ran out to the accompaniment of my squeals! I was glad when the beets were all collected in the truck.

We were poor in those days. It takes years of sacrificing to acquire machinery, and the cash returns on crops never seemed to catch up with the year's expenses for gas, seed, labour and day-to-day living. Yet the poverty never affected us adversely, and we managed to have a good life.

We had a large old house and several times shared it with the family we had hired to work our beets. Some of these people were immigrants, too, and couldn't speak English. Sometimes they arrived with few possessions, their household goods still *en route* from Holland or Germany. We'd loan them cookware, cutlery and even furniture, although we had barely enough ourselves. We are still friendly with some of these families, and it has been interesting to watch their progress and their gradual Canadianization.

One year we had a family of quiet and industrious Crees from Saskatchewan: a grandmother, daughter, daughter-in-law and two small children. They were used to going barefoot, and it was the first time I saw wood for the fire broken by bare feet. The grandmother was the widow of a former chief and she used to regale us with stories of her youth. She told about the young braves coming home from raiding sorties with scalps. She was inured to hardship and not comfortable sleeping in a bed, preferring to sleep on the floor.

Looking back on those early days, the rest seems almost anti-climactic. We gradually acquired some prosperity and eventually left the farm which we'd modernized, installing gas, electricity, running water and oh, heavenly day, a flush toilet! That convenience meant no more dressing up in parka and overshoes for a trip to the outhouse in winter.

I shall not forget the rural life with the community showers, the box socials, gravel roads and dances at the school, not to mention the work from dawn to dusk. But once the harvest was in, there were the cosy winter evenings spent around the old coal stove, games to play, books to read and jigsaw puzzles to do together. Anyone who has never lived the country life has missed a great experience.

The scene changed constantly. The soft rolling hills of Manitoba, tufted here and there with billowing trees, reminded me of the English downs. In Saskatchewan the miles of barren flat lands flowed into infinity. Empty wheat fields bleakly waited for the first fall of snow. At Edmonton, Alberta, the train made an hour long stop-over. We took our breakfast in the station restaurant, and I stared wide-eyed at cowboys wearing tight jeans and Stetson hats. I had only seen them in films.

The foothills of Alberta sprouted eventually into the awesome peaks of the Rocky Mountains. The train climbed steadily until it appeared it could go no higher and then in the midst of craggy pinnacles, miles from nowhere, it came to a hissing stop. I thought to myself, it's finally given up the ghost. Actually, it had stopped to give passengers an opportunity to get out and look at Mount Robson, the highest mountain in Canada. Our next stop was Jasper Park and from there it was down hill all the way to our destination, Kamloops, British Columbia.

We were to be met in Kamloops by the Smiths, Bill's sister and husband. It was meeting I viewed with some trepidation. How would they like me and how would I like them?

As we stepped off the train I heard a man's voice say, "There they are." As I turned, a man and woman walked up to us. The man was in his early forties, his face tanned and weather-worn. The woman I recognized immediately as Bill's sister. She had the same finely-cut features and dark brown curly hair. I remember thinking that she was quite beautiful if one looked beneath the premature lines that creased her face. Two pleasant people dressed in the simple manner that suggested they were farmers.

As I climbed into the back seat of their '29 Buick, something snapped inside me. They were talking, but I couldn't answer. The car sped into the night and I leaned against Bill. The tears came quickly and quietly. Whether I liked it or not I was almost home, among total strangers and far from father, mother and sister. How was I to know then that the fun was only beginning.

The homesickness had begun and was to continue for many years. In letters home I told of my exciting experiences, but much later, when my mother came to Canada, she told me how father had read between the lines. "Eileen is unhappy," he'd said.

My husband's family lived in Vernon, B.C., and for a time we stayed with his parents and younger sister. The Smith's lived across the road with their four children, while his brother and wife lived three miles away. The family tried to make me feel welcome, but from the outset it was plain that there was a vast social difference between their lifestyle and mine. They were small farmers, kindly folk, and were very concerned about the basic requirements of life. There seemed to be neither the time nor the money to spend on the type of entertainment I'd grown accustomed to in England.

I realized quickly that life in Vernon was hard and that it took a certain toughness to survive. There were many material benefits such as cars, homes and fancy electrical appliances. Yet beneath the surface I saw that people of my age had not experienced the more worldly educational opportunities that I had taken for granted.

I missed Worthing, a summer resort town with miles of flower bedecked promenades along its seafront. I missed the nights at the theatre and being able to choose between four cinemas. I missed the orderly streets and tidy gardens. Most of all I missed father's antique shop, where I'd helped him. I missed his fine tenor voice in the yearly Gilbert and Sullivan musicals. And I missed our musical friends. Suddenly, all I heard were cowboy songs, and they nearly drove me out of my mind.

The sophisticated life was being replaced by a new set of values. Why did you bring me here, was my question. But, like it or not, one thing I would not do was to admit to my father that I might have been wrong or to go running home, suitcase in hand.

I don't wish to give the impression that I was entirely unhappy in this land of hot summers and cold winters. That would not be true. I knew that my husband loved me and I could not foresee life with any other. And I realized that he would be happier working in his own homeland. I could compromise. At the occasional family get-togethers when the discussion centred around the latest method of raising hogs or the best way to preserve beans, I'd remain a silent listener. Eventually I'd excuse myself and while away the time with a few tunes on the old family piano.

With spring came the promise of new adventure. Bill had been working with the forestry department and learned that he'd be going to Silver Star Mountain as a lookout during the fire season. By this time we'd bought our first car—the Smith's old '29 Buick—for $250, I think. One day in June we loaded it with groceries, bedding and a few pots and pans and left for our mountain home.

The old car puffed and boiled its way up the tortuous, winding incline over gravel, mud and rocks. By the roadside a showy hue of wild flowers budded and blossomed. The glass-walled cabin built at the summit, 6000 feet above sea level, overlooked miles of surrounding bushland. Bill's job was to look for any tell-tale sign of smoke and report its location over the two-way radio. At 8:00 a.m. each morning he'd roll out of bed and switch it on. We'd listen as each lookout gave his signal and morning report.

During the day we'd hike through bush and plateaus, always on the look-out for that wisp of smoke. It was at this mountain retreat that I first came into contact with the outhouse—a bone-chilling structure I was to come across again and again in the years to come.

I also saw my first deer, and my first coyote. I never actually saw a bear on Silver Star but I knew they were there. One day I heard a great shuffling and shaking among the huckleberry bushes. "Stay near the cabin," said Bill. "The bears are down over the hill eating the berries."

My worst experience on the mountain was during a thunderstorm. I have never seen such fury as that night. I cowered under the bed, hands over my head, as lightning zigzagged off the rocks outside and blue lights flashed and bounced off the cooking stove. The thunder roared and rolled around us, and I thought the mountain would split in two. Later, I crawled out from under the bed to the tune of my husband's laughter.

A great stillness engulfed us most of the time, but although we were the only humans for miles around, I never felt alone. Visitors sometimes ventured to our haven, usually on a Sunday, and the forest warden made annual trips to check on us. Then it was time to pack and come down out of the clouds. Thick damp mists had begun to shroud our retreat, and days were growing colder. Soon the snows would come, and the road would be impassable. I had lived in the Canadian mountains and found them not unfriendly. Why then did I dream of walking once again upon the Sussex Downs?

For the next two years we lived in Vernon. Our son was born and we named him after the town. He was a year old when we decided to head out again so that Bill could join a logging crew. We went to live in Minto, a small town accessible only by train from Lillooet. We lived in a one-bedroom house and had to carry all our water from the old hotel down the one street. There was one general store and a post office, and mail delivery was at the whim of a cantankerous old lady who sensed the power she wielded in that small place.

I was quite happy to be out in the mountains again. The loggers were a new breed, a happy-go-lucky bunch who worked and played hard. I added new words to my vocabulary, words such as whistle punk, donkey engine and spar tree. I learned the importance of the local beer parlour and in time I managed to down a few glasses with the best of them. It was a carefree summer with good times, but inevitably the weather changed, making operations impossible. I was soon to understand the full significance of the words "laid off". We went back to Bill's parents and spent an uneventful winter.

The following summer found us in the Sechelt Peninsula. At last our wanderings had brought us to the coast of British Columbia. I had longed to see Vancouver, the big city, and when I did I knew that we had to live there some day. Theatres and department stores were once again within reach. But this time our visit was short.

In just two days we were off again, to the campsite where we were to spend the summer with four other families and the rest of the loggers. The work camp consisted of a bunkhouse, cookshack and workshops. Like the other families, we lived in a twelve-by-fourteen-foot tent. Complete with stove and beds, it was quite comfortable. The camp was on the shoreline of Salmon Inlet, and at high tide we'd be completely cut off, an island unto ourselves.

By now, our son Vernon was toddling around and was accustomed to seeing raccoons and the occasional bear. In July and August the weather was too hot for the men to continue their work in the bush. The brush was tinder dry, and there was the ever present threat of fire. The men were given jobs elsewhere, and Bill was put in charge of the company motor launch, a thirty-foot vessel with all facilities. We lived aboard the *Lucy C* for two months and enjoyed every minute.

It was a time of great tranquility. The beauty and grandeur of the coastal waterways left little to be desired. When the fire season was over, we went back to the camp until fall. One day Bill came home announcing he'd been laid off again. I still found it hard to understand fully the way things were done in this country. "What will we do?" I asked. He held me close. "Don't worry I've got faith, we'll be all right." And I believed him.

We spent the winter in Vancouver and because we couldn't find anything better, we took a two-room apartment in a seedy area off Hastings Street. Today I shudder when I think of it. It had a dank, depressing atmosphere and cockroaches roamed the cupboards at night. One toilet served four apartments. There was no bath. The walls were paper thin, and the man and woman who lived next door would get drunk and argue. I think he hit her sometimes. He was much younger than she, and we surmised that she was a prostitute and he her pimp. In another apartment on our floor someone was knifed. But the final outrage came one warm sunny afternoon while I was sitting by the window. A big car drove up, and a middle-aged man looked up and smiled. For a moment I was puzzled. He came up the hall steps and knocked on the door. Then the awful truth burst through my subconscious like a floodtide. Oh, no! It couldn't be. He didn't think. . . . As I opened the door to his leering face I knew he was there for only one reason. My English discipline came to the fore. Stony-faced and curt I sent him packing.

The sordidness of our surroundings wore me down to a point where I became sick. I had a complete physical, but the doctor could only conclude that I was suffering from nerves. I'd think of my home in England furnished with delicate antiques, the walls hung with my father's paintings, and a wave of nostalgia would sweep over me and I'd weep. I found the contrast almost too much to endure. I don't know how much longer I could have stood it. Then relief came. Bill received word from his union office to report for a job at Trail and the Waneta Dam site.

We bought the plane tickets and flew to Trail. Talk about having faith—we arrived there broke. The company had supplied Bill's plane fare and there was a place for him in the bunkhouse at the job site. For Vernon and me there was nothing. We had no car and we were penniless.

We found a hotel and Bill told the manager of our plight. He agreed to let us have a room, and Bill would pay when he received his wages. We had a roof over our heads, but how would we eat for the next two weeks? Bill tried again. "I've found a Chinese cafe down the street. They'll allow you and Vernon to eat your meals there and I'll pay later. All you have to do is sign the check stub." That night, I whispered a prayer of thanks.

We soon realized that the money Bill would be making at Waneta would be the most he'd made thus far and there'd be lots of overtime.

Most of the workers and their families had set up a camp in a farmer's field near the dam construction site. It was on the Canadian-U.S. border a few miles south of Trail. We sent for our tent and few belongings, paid the farmer ten dollars a month for a spot and moved in. We set the tent up, building a wooden floor and three-foot high walls. We insulated the walls, built cupboards, purchased an oil stove and furnished it cosily. About two dozen families were living there in much the same way as we were. The men had built a shower stall, outside toilets and had piped water from a creek on the property.

The life of the construction worker was very similar to that of a logger. They, too, worked and played hard. There was a kind of camaraderie among us, for we were all outsiders who didn't fit in with the townspeople. The work was dangerous: there were accidents and even deaths. A bulldozer working near the edge of the cliff plummeted down hundreds of feet to be crushed on the rocks below. Another time a man fell to his death in the raging waters of the Columbia River.

We women spent our days visiting back and forth, doing the cooking and chores, carrying our buckets of water across the field and waiting for the men to come home.

Four years had passed since I had arrived in Canada, and I still found it hard to relate to the people. Something was wrong, but I couldn't put my finger on it. I tried to think and act like the women I met every day. I really *wanted* to belong. I'd had a close association with theatre in England and perhaps I was acting out a kind of charade. I made myself over, became someone I really was not, until I seemed to be neither one thing nor the other. I tried to please yet pleased no one. I lost my identity and the complex problem remained with me a long time.

Our gypsy life continued as we moved from Waneta to Tye. At last we were getting on our financial feet. We had another car and a twenty-five-foot house trailer. Tye was another isolated area, and access to it was gained either by taking the train from Creston or by crossing the Kooteney Lake. Our trailer was taken in on a barge, water lapping at its wheels.

Located by the lake, the logging camp was in a particularly wild place and plagued by black bears. All summer long they broke into the cook's meat cooler. Cooky would often trudge up the road in the evening, gun under arm, muttering to anyone within earshot, "I'll get those ?!%$#& bears if it's the last thing I do." He'd disappear toward the garbage dump where the bears gathered in large numbers, fire a few shots in the air and come back down feeling a little better.

One hot afternoon a bear wandered out of the bush and stood looking through the screen door of our trailer. My son and I were alone. Vernon was frightened. I picked him up, stood my ground and addressed the bear: "Shoo, go on, get out of here." He gave a lazy grunt and to my great relief, waddled off.

Winter came and once again there was no work. Overnight it seemed that the men were gone and the camp deserted. The owners had agreed to pay the cost of taking us out but had not kept their promise. We had no money to get our trailer out by flatcar so we stayed on. Snow came. We had water, but food was scarce. Bill went off into the hills and came back with a deer. We hung it in one of the work shacks where it froze. In time the unemployment cheques came through, but without that deer I think we'd have starved.

When the warm February sun brought the run off, we wondered what we would do. By then I had developed the attitude of sitting back and waiting for something to happen. Sure enough, it wasn't long before we had a visitor—one of the owners. He hooked up our trailer, put us on a flatcar and took us back to town. We arrived in Creston station late in the evening and were told that the trailer could not be taken off until early morning.

We had a meal in town and decided to go back and sleep in the trailer to save hotel fees. The trailer was on the flatcar on a siding, way up the track. We got inside and went right to bed. I was awoken from sleep by a rumbling sound. For a moment I wondered where I was, then realized it must be a train passing through on the main line.

I dropped off into a fitful sleep. Again I woke with a start. It was a train. The noise was deafening and the trailer was shaking again. I checked on Vernon; he was sleeping peacefully. By this time dishes were rattling in the cupboards. Something fell down on my bare foot. I grabbed at the edge of the front window and looked out. The bright light of a locomotive was bearing down on us. My years of living in wartime England had taught me one thing—in the face of impending disaster, get down on the floor and stay there. Old habits took over, I was down there on all fours, hands over ears. I caught a fleeting glimpse of Bill sitting on the bed struggling to get into his pants. There was a resounding crash as the engine hit us and a terrific jolt.

Our flatcar was freewheeling it down the track, and we were travelling so fast that I thought we'd take off into space. Finally, we stopped, miles from the station. It was very quiet and very dark. We checked Vernon again (he'd mercifully slept through it all) and eventually dozed off—this time fully clothed.

Once more I awakened to a low rumbling which got louder and louder. The train stopped, and I lay there holding my breath, straining for any new sound. Chains clanked, there was a thud, a squeak and a jerk, and then we were off again being pulled back down the track.

I shook Bill. "Wake up! It's started again!" He sat up. "Why can't they leave us alone?" "If they knew we were here, they might," I suggested. Bill decided to open the door and wave his white shirt at the brakey who was hanging on to the engine. The man gave a strangled cry, jumped from the slowly moving engine and bolted down the track as fast as his legs would carry him, past the train and disappeared in the direction of town.

"I think we must have startled him," said Bill. We looked at one another and began to laugh.

In the cold of pre-dawn awakening we dressed our still sleepy son and ventured down the track to our car. We sat there until the cafe opened for breakfast.

Our son was near school age, and we knew that our days of wandering must end. We moved to Cranbrook where Bill was to start work with the telephone company. We found a small home to rent and settled down as respectable citizens, becoming involved in the town's activities. Bill became vice president of the National Film Board group in Cranbrook, and I was elected its treasurer. He joined the Air Force Reserve and was Commander of the Air Cadets. The church played an important role in our lives and I worked as Sunday School Secretary, among other things. I was finding it easier to relate to others and developing my own personality.

In time the company moved Bill to Vancouver and I was delighted. This was where I had always wanted to live. We bought our first small home on Capitol Hill and our daughter, Victoria, was born in Vancouver General Hospital. When my mother and sister came out from England my world seemed complete. But my happiness was brief. Within six weeks my sister decided not to make her home in Canada and returned to England. Nine months later my mother was dead.

I was grief stricken, my spirits were lower than they had ever been. I blamed my husband, I blamed Canada and all I had endured which had brought me to this. Those nine years when I had missed seeing her and now I'd never see her again. I cried myself to sleep every night for almost a year. Then one night she appeared to me in a dream and told me not to grieve any more. From that time on I found a new strength and peace.

When our daughter was twelve we took her to England to visit uncles, aunts and cousins (my father had long since gone to live in Africa). It was fun, but when it was over I knew that I no longer belonged there. I was a naturalized Canadian, my mind had broadened, my scope of thought had changed—expanded if you like. In Britain they still seemed to be piling the crumbling rocks of tradition one upon the other. When I landed on Canadian soil for the second time I knew I had come home to stay.

Home and Homesickness

Homesickness is one of those insidious maladies which attacks, then retreats, then waits for another weakness in the defence and attacks again. In the 1940s an epidemic of homesickness attacked thousands of unwary war brides.

Was there a war bride who could deny knowledge of that searing nostalgia? A small percentage were overwhelmed by it and returned home. The rest lived with it until time eased the pangs. For some it still lurks, ready for an occasional skirmish.

It began before I left home. Mind you, there was no question but that I'd go to Canada and I was eager to get there to join my husband. Then it suddenly hit me. I was leaving my native land and all its beauty and customs. I was leaving all those people I loved and who loved me. One of my girl friends remarked, "You shouldn't leave England, you're so English." I sobbed off and on for three days and nights before I left.

Friends of the family took me to catch the train at New-haven, Sussex, for the first stage of my journey. They helped me regain my composure. The trip and the first few weeks in Canada were full of excitement and new experiences.

But soon the homesickness took hold again. I missed the sea, its sound, the spray and the southwest winds. I missed a lot of people and a lot of things. I think I felt the classic wretchedness of the emigrant. I did more crying and was likely considered something of an ingrate and an oddball, although it was through no fault of Canada or Canadians. An ex-Lancashire lady told me that it would take at least ten years to get over the yearning.

As I became busier with successive children, the homesickness was reined in and delegated to some dark, quiet recess of my mind. It manages to get loose occasionally even now, and plays havoc with my Canadianization. For me, homesickness is all mixed up with youth and carefree days, the sea and South Downs, history and heritage.

No doctor can prescribe for homesickness. It's a terrible malady. You fight to rid your being of the damned thing but you really only suppress it.

Homesickness hits you below the belt. It sneaks up on you in a song, a line of poetry or a smell. Burning leaves and newly-cut grass brings tears to my eyes, reminding me of our garden and my dad tending it.

You learn how to adjust to its sharp nostalgic twinges. You sort of trap it and confine it again to the back of your mind.

It's Christmas now, I'm always more homesick at this time of year for things that are gone. No use letting it get the better of me, but I'll be English until I die.

For years, homesickness would suddenly overwhelm me. It was a decade before I entered an Anglican church, and then I sobbed throughout the service. And for years I cried every time the weekly letter from my mother arrived. She kept writing until the age of ninety-two, and I hoard her letters still.

It took me a long time to get over homesickness. Before I came to Canada I had never been further than London, about sixty miles away, on my own. I tried to write happy letters home to my people, but they detected my unhappiness.

I did enjoy the abundance of food and often popped into ice cream parlours for servings of strawberry shortcake. But how I missed the pubs, English tomatoes and bread, and most of all, the sea.

I recall that the day after I arrived, a friend of my husband's family came to call. She told me that she had been a war bride from the First World War. I couldn't imagine why she had stayed all those years. Now here I am, having stayed thirty years myself.

My first impressions of Canada were clouded with disappointment, frustration and a terrible homesickness. It took me about a year to get over that. Imagine leaving a place with a population of 135,000 and moving to Amherst, Nova Scotia, population 9000 at the time. I thought that I was still in the country when we arrived there from Halifax. However, I soon adapted and when I take a trip to England now, I get homesick for Canada.

Homesickness has never really ceased for me, although it's not as painful as it once was.

I don't think I could go back there to live in England now, and that is not because of any material reasons. It is simply that England is not the England of my recollections. Times, people and places change. There's no going back.

My memories are pleasant ones and in my mind I always see it in summer, green and beautiful, as only Sussex can be. The sun sparkles on the sea and there are picnics and good times. Grey skies, pouring rain, cold bedrooms and all the rest—they just don't occur in my reveries.

Some war brides turned back at the ships. Others made the trip but eventually returned to Europe, homesick or disappointed. Although happiness had eluded them in Canada, many of these women remember the country and its people with deep affection.

How overjoyed I'd be if this could be a story about a happy life spent in Canada.

At the age of nineteen and against my parents' wishes, I married a charming Canadian from Lachine in Quebec. Our baby son was born a year later.

At the end of the war, my husband returned home. I, along with many other war brides, waited to follow. I remember buying new clothes, having my papers in order, packing suitcases and even rising on the day of departure with great joy. Alas, my parents won. To this day and for always, my lack of courage will be with me.

This is not self-pity but rather guilt for having deprived my son of his father and a father of his son. My son has grown to be a fine person, enjoying a successful career and a happy family.

Mine is a story in reverse to those of most of the war brides. I intend to visit Canada one day and maybe find peace of mind.

I arrived in Canada with great hopes, looking forward to rejoining my husband and to our new life together. We had one little girl aged three and a half, and I was expecting another baby, born four months after I landed.

Many of the English-speaking people of Drummondville, Quebec, were very kind to the newly arrived war brides. They welcomed us and made us feel more at home. But, with two small children, it was often difficult for me to join in social activities. Like lots of other war brides, I had never been away from home and family for any length of time before. I got terribly homesick.

I realized that not knowing French was a decided drawback. Most of the families on our street were French speaking. Anne played with the children and picked up some of the language. I think I was too self-conscious to try. Perhaps I could have made friends with my neighbours if I had been able to communicate. Some seemed friendly but rather timid. Like me, I suppose.

My husband did his very best to help me settle in, but I just couldn't make it. When I found I was pregnant again I felt that I had to get back home. Perhaps, if the Pill had been available then, life might not have seemed so complicated.

My husband was wonderful about it all, and I have never regretted coming back to England. I had wanted to go to Canada and I am really glad that I went. While we realized that we would have to work hard for a living wherever we lived, we felt the main thing was to be as happy as possible.

I sailed on the *Aquitania* with hundreds of other war brides in June 1946. I remember there were forty-four of us in the cabin.

I arrived in London, Ontario, on July 1 in blazing sunshine. London was a lovely place known as "the forest city", within easy reach of the summer resorts, Grand Bend, Ipperwash Beach and Port Stanley.

I spent fifteen years there and then my marriage broke up. Pressures were put on me to return with my children to Britain. My doctor advised the same course. At the time it seemed the best thing to do. Later, when I realized that it really wasn't the answer, it was no longer possible for me to return to Canada.

Twelve years afterwards I heard my husband was dead. The saddest thing was that my eldest daughter had asked him to come over to England that summer.

If I could afford it, I should love to return to London, Ontario, at least for a visit. But what changes would I find? Perhaps my memories would be spoiled.

A visit to the homeland is a bitter-sweet experience for emigrants and exiles. Everything has changed, yet seems to have remained the same. Familiar people, places and things are quickly assimilated and added to memory along with scenes of youth. Nostalgia, disappointment and delight; the mixture of emotions with which the war brides had greeted the new land was there again for their return to the old.

How different the port [Liverpool] looked this time: planes wheeling overhead, docks a hive of activity, great liners anchored nearby, a fleet of double-decker buses lined up at the ferry and, most striking of all, the spires of the cathedral rising above the rooftops as a symbol of faith and courage.

As the boat train sped towards London I glued my eyes to the window and thought, "It's good to be back in England's green and pleasant land."

The beauty of London in June seemed like a miracle to one who had been away. Such a mingling of light and colour. The bright green of the trees and grass, the grey stones and scarlet buses shining in the suffused sun. Across the trim acres of a park the familiar sounds of London—a roar of traffic, music of a barrel organ and cries of news vendors—brought back so many happy memories.

It was while standing outside the superb towers and terraces of Windsor Castle, watching the Guards march up and down in their red tunics and bearskins, that I remembered the words of another war bride. She had written to a Vancouver newspaper that from six thousand miles away you view England through rose colored glasses but to come home means disillusionment. Well, I had come home and far from being disillusioned it seemed as if only now had I ever worn glasses. The scenes which merely impressed me before now moved me to the verge of tears. After three years in Northern Ontario I was seeing my homeland as if for the first time.

And so I took my fill of all things lovely. Shady chestnut trees around village greens, great clusters of pinky-blue hydrangeas, lawns smooth as velvet, fragrant lavender in cottage gardens, bird song in the early morning. During the long, cold Canadian winters I would remember all these things.

One incident during the visit stamped itself very vividly on my mind. Less than a week after American Independence Day I happened to be in Grosvenor Square and wandered along to see the memorial to President Roosevelt. There was a solitary wreath at the foot of the statue. Curiously I went to have a closer look. On a card attached to the fading lilies and gladioli I read: "In memory of a great gentleman." It was signed, "A forgotten G.I. bride."

One evening about a month after arriving in London I had a phone call from a war bride who had come over on the same ship. She was a dark-haired, very attractive girl who had served in the WRNS during the war. That was how she had met her husband, then in the Canadian Navy. Her cabin on board ship was next to mine and we became good friends. Her two-year-old boy loved to play with my three boys.

She often told me, as we watched our children play, of her happiness in Canada. She loved the country and the people. Just at first it had not been easy. They were living in one room and she had worked for a while to help their finances. And then, like so many war brides in a new land, she had lost her health.

But that was back in the past. Now they had a nice apartment, her husband a good job, and they both adored their tiny son. Her one regret was the parting from her husband while making this visit to her parents in England.

A few days after parting in London, she phoned me to learn if my children were all right. Her small son had developed measles. I remember her words before ringing off: "Now that I've seen my parents and old acquaintances I can hardly wait to get back to Canada."

But this time her voice was full of distress. She had received a cable, an air letter and finally a telephone call from her husband in Toronto. He had found someone else and never wanted to see his wife and son again. Within the hour we had arranged to meet and were walking around Oxford Circus. She was in a complete daze and kept repeating, "This must be happening in a film. I can't believe it's true." Later as we sipped hot coffee in a restaurant, she came to a decision. She was going back to Canada—and the sooner the better. She would get back somehow, although her money would only take her to Quebec. She still loved her husband enough to want to return and, if only for the sake of her son, she would fight to save her marriage. And even if that failed she felt that Canada was her country now. If she had to go out to work there were better opportunities there than in the Old Country.

The last few weeks in England passed all too quickly and soon it was time to get my little family ready for the long journey home to Canada. I dreaded the inevitable parting from my parents and could understand one war bride saying that she thought this alone would keep her in Canada. Never again would she return to England and face the ordeal of saying goodbye to her parents. When you know that an ocean divides and that years may pass before you meet again—if you ever do meet again—then it's not easy to say farewell.

When our ship arrived in Liverpool the sun shone from a clear blue sky, everyone was on deck waving madly towards the shore and the excitement was intense. Joy seemed to radiate all around. But on the day of leaving England the skies were grey and a miserable drizzle of rain soaked the bedraggled crowd of relatives huddled disconsolately on the quayside. Surely these goodbyes are among the worst moments in life. . . .

From "This is the life" by Gwyneth M. Shirley, first published in *New Liberty Magazine*, June, 1952.

I love to visit England but doubt that I could enjoy living there again. For one thing I'd miss the friendly chatter of strangers. It's too bad that the great spirit of informality so obvious during the war, somehow disappeared again when peace came.

On visits to the U.K. I have been amazed at the lack of knowledge and lack of interest in Canada. Life has changed over there, and I doubt if we'd fit in now.

The scenery is wonderful, but on my first return visit my mother reacted to my homesickness by saying, "Scenery is scenery, you can't live on scenery."

My Canadian friends think that England is marvellous, all those historical buildings, the roses, the quaint pubs, the thatched cottages, the London theatre shows, the Guards and so on.

Each time I go back home I am disappointed. The country seems to be going downhill. My first impression of London in 1972 was the dirt and litter on such famous streets as Oxford and Regent and the underground stations. The Wimpy Bars, where one might stop for a quick snack were filthy, both in London or Edinburgh. The commercialism at Westminster, Salisbury, Windsor, Stratford—I found it heartbreaking and degrading.

Even after thirty years I don't look at Britain from a Canadian point of view. My eyes are still those of a concerned native daughter.

I went back for a visit in 1966 and found out what a lot of changes there had been. Old landmarks had disappeared and primrose lanes had been torn up to make traffic lay-bys. And then there were the changes in myself. It was terribly sad to find that I no longer had anything in common with old dear friends. I am not a negative person but on my return, I told my husband that I wouldn't go back again.

In spite of dire prophesies at the beginning, Canada has been good to me. I have a good husband and a stable marriage.

During my visits back to England, and I've been a few times since my family grew up, I have split loyalties. I love the country of my birth and youth but feel that I couldn't live there very comfortably now. My thirty years in Canada have changed me and the England I remember from childhood has vanished. I feel that the pace of life is a little slower there and the children tend to be better mannered. But for me, something seems to be missing and I want to get back to Alberta where I really feel at home.

Appendix

On December 31, 1946, a total of 69,733 dependents were recorded. The break-down by countries was as follows:

	Wives	Children
Great Britain	44,886	21,358
Holland	1,886	428
Belgium	649	131
France	100	15
Italy	26	10
Denmark	7	1
Germany	6	2
Norway	1	
North Africa	1	
South Africa	1	
Greece	1	
Algiers	1	
Hungary		3
Russia	1	
India	1	
Malay	2	
Australia	24	2
Newfoundland and Carribean Area	190	
	47,783	21,950

Dependents were divided roughly by the following percentages according to the services in which the husbands served:

	Wives	Children
Army	80	85.5
RCAF	18	13.1
Navy	2	1.4

Research References: *Public Archives of Canada*

File HQ 54-27-1-58 (Record Group 24, volume 2052)
File HQ 650-124-33 (Record Group 24, volume 6545)
File HQS 8536-1 (Record Group 24, microfilm reel C-5520)
Immigration Branch File (Record Group 76, volumes 460-462, file 705870)

Acknowledgements

Thanks are due and gratefully given to all those who encouraged and helped me to complete this project—first and foremost my family and my friends.

Special acknowledgement goes to the following individuals and organizations for their assistance.

Lorne Manchester, past Editor, *Legion Magazine*
Jane Dewar, Editor, *Legion Magazine*
The Canadian Red Cross Society, Montreal Branch
CBC Radio Programme "As It Happens," Personal
    Classifieds
The Public Archives, Ottawa
Barbara Wilson, Military Specialist, State and Military
    Records Section, Public Records Division, Historical
    Records Branch, Public Archives, Ottawa
The many Canadian newspaper editors and those in the
    United Kingdom who kindly published my letters asking
    readers for information
Barry Broadfoot, whose book *Six War Years 1939-1945*
    provided the necessary impetus to transform an
    incubating idea into the actual search for war brides' own
    stories
International Women's Year

Sincere thanks go to the following war brides who so generously contributed their stories and/or photographs. Thanks also to those who wrote from Britain and to those who declined to be named here.

Nan Archibald, Saskatoon, Saskatchewan.
Joyce Astrop, Oshawa, Ontario.
Celia Beach, Weyburn, Saskatchewan.
Kay Béland, Franklin Centre, Quebec.
Betty Bernier, Chateauguay, Quebec.

Renée Blue, Kingston, Ontario.
Jessie Bowes, Lethbridge, Alberta.
Kitty Boucher, Red Deer, Alberta.
Gloria Brock, Abernethy, Saskatchewan.
Mary Collins, Airdrie, Scotland.
Phyllis Cook, Shoreham-by-Sea, England.
Laura Cottrell, Prince Albert, Saskatchewan.
Eleanor Cringan, Victoria, British Columbia.
Doris Dailey, St. Catharines, Ontario.
Win Desjardins, Ottawa, Ontario.
Barbara Durant, Brockville, Ontario.
Vera Dustin, Golden, British Columbia.
Betty Faris, Aylmer, Quebec.
Joan Fitzgibbon, Sussex, England.
Alice Frenette, Fort Frances, Ontario.
Joyce Gilchrist, Melbourne, Quebec.
Molly Green, Winnipeg, Manitoba.
Betty Hawkins, Fredericton, New Brunswick.
Norah Hawn, Lethbridge, Alberta.
Marjorie Hopkins, Sydney Mines, Nova Scotia.
Pauline Hunter, Amherst, Nova Scotia.
Wilhelmina Jones, Ste. Thérèse, Quebec.
Faith Kenyon, Lloydminster, Saskatchewan.
Betty Killingbeck, Peterborough, Ontario.
Connie Kingerlee, Sidney, British Columbia.
Miriam Kirkpatrick, Embro, Ontario.
Kathleen Lauzière, Drummondville, Quebec.
Sheila Laird, Toronto, Ontario.
Rita Lepage, Rimouski, Quebec.
Marjorie Lindsay, Winnipeg, Manitoba.
Marjorie MacWilliams, Sidney, British Columbia.
Irene Maio, Peterborough, Ontario.
Joyce Marshall, London, Ontario.
Ellen Messier, Drummondville, Quebec.
Hilda Minshall, Birmingham, England.
Hilda Mitcheltree, Head of Jeddore, Nova Scotia.
Hilda Mleczko, Glace Bay, Nova Scotia.

Dorothy Peacock, London, Ontario.
Lilian Pearson, Birsay, Saskatchewan.
Ruby Pearson, Victoria, British Columbia.
Nancy Poffley, Kingston, Ontario.
Nancy Poupart, Calgary, Alberta.
Peg Robinson, Winnipeg, Manitoba.
Norma Salter, Stellarton, Nova Scotia.
Eileen Shaw, Quesnel, British Columbia.
Gwyneth Shirley, Cochrane, Ontario.
Iris Simpson, Red Deer, Alberta.
Helene Smith, Glaslyn, Saskatchewan.
Daphne Tribe, Hove, England.
Mollie Watt, Victoria, British Columbia.
Margaret White, Worthing, England.
Jean Williams, Clive, Alberta.
Sarah Wilson, Kitchener, Ontario.
Lorill Wingrave, Millet, Alberta.
Mary Wood, Kingsbury, Quebec.

[MOA317 8=VALLEYFIELD QUE 28 456P

MRS J K HIBBERT, CARE

DUE HALIFAX TOMO

WELCOME TO CANADA JOYC

DAD ELSIE JOS.

AFT CABIN.

FIRST SITTING.

Table No......11

Seat No.............

Name................

Passengers are requested to hand this card to the Table
Steward when taking their seat at first meal.

TO EXAMINING OFFICIALS:

THE BEARER

MRS JOYCE KATHLEEN HIBBE

is travelling to Canada under the
Scheme of the Canadian Governr
wives, widows and children of me
Canadian Forces Overseas.

PASSPORT AND PERMIT OFFICE.

EXIT PERMIT № 35624

Valid for departure before
12 October 1945
and for one journey only.

Holder is travelling to:
Canada.

DIRECT OR VIA U.S.

IN TRANSIT ONL